The Fiction Writer's Guide to Alternate History

The Fiction Writer's Guide to Alternate History

A Handbook on Craft, Art, and History

Jack Dann

BLOOMSBURY ACADEMIC
LONDON • NEW YORK • OXFORD • NEW DELHI • SYDNEY

BLOOMSBURY ACADEMIC
Bloomsbury Publishing Plc
50 Bedford Square, London, WC1B 3DP, UK
1385 Broadway, New York, NY 10018, USA
29 Earlsfort Terrace, Dublin 2, Ireland

BLOOMSBURY, BLOOMSBURY ACADEMIC and the Diana logo
are trademarks of Bloomsbury Publishing Plc

First published in Great Britain 2023

Cover design and illustration by Rebecca Heselton
Textures © Dorothy Gaziano/Shutterstock

A catalogue record for this book is available from the British Library.

Library of Congress Cataloging-in-Publication Data
Names: Dann, Jack, author.
Title: The fiction writer's guide to alternate history : a handbook on craft,
art, and history / Jack Dann.
Description: London ; New York : Bloomsbury Academic, 2023. | Includes
bibliographical references and index.
Identifiers: LCCN 2022055784 (print) | LCCN 2022055785 (ebook) |
ISBN 9781350351356 (hardback) | ISBN 9781350351363 (paperback) |
ISBN 9781350351370 (pdf) | ISBN 9781350351387 (epub)
Subjects: LCSH: Alternative histories (Fiction)–Authorship.
Classification: LCC PN3377.5.A48 D36 2023 (print) | LCC PN3377.5.A48
(ebook) | DDC 808.3/8768–dc23/eng/20230210
LC record available at https://lccn.loc.gov/2022055784
LC ebook record available at https://lccn.loc.gov/2022055785

ISBN: HB: 978-1-3503-5135-6
         PB: 978-1-3503-5136-3
         ePDF: 978-1-3503-5137-0
         eBook: 978-1-3503-5138-7

Typeset by Integra Software Services Pvt. Ltd.
Printed and bound in Great Britain

To find out more about our authors and books visit www.bloomsbury.com
and sign up for our newsletters.

This book is dedicated to the memory of Mary Freeman Rosenblum ...

CONTENTS

ILLUSTRATIONS

1

A Few Introductory Notes and Thoughts about Alternate History and the Slippery Slope of Fiction

Fiction—any kind of fiction, whatever the genre, whatever its pretensions or subject-matter—is a rule-based enterprise; and we writers take great delight in bending, stretching, twisting, and breaking the rules. It's part of how art and craft evolve. Keep in mind, though, that most evolutionary experiments end in failure ... and breaking the rules before you know the rules is probably *not* a good survival strategy!

Fiction is a constructed reality of conventions (a less provocative term than rules) that both readers and writers accept. That's why when we read dialogue, we don't get put off by the repetitive "he said" and "she said." They are clarification indicators and do not obstruct the flow of the dialogue because we simply accept them as a literary convention. In essence, they become a form of punctuation. But when novice writers begin writing line-by-line dialogue, they often go to extreme lengths *not* to be repetitive because the "he said," "she said," and "they said" (the last can also be read as an evolving social/literary convention) often just *look* wrong. So the novice tries to resolve the perceived awkwardness by resorting to dreaded "saidbookisms" such as "she ejaculated" (ouch!), "he enthused," "she guffawed," "they sighed" ... and on and on. And, as mentioned earlier in a parenthetical, as social norms change, so do literary conventions.

If we are to stay current, we need to keep up with the ... rules. I mean conventions.

I will tell you what those conventions are for the counterfactual fiction genre, and I'll also take some time specifying exactly what we're talking about. If you want to write alternate history with authority, it helps to know what's been done in the genre—to actually know the history and shape of the genre (split-infinitive intentional!)—so you don't keep trying to reinvent the wheel by using primitive tropes and ideas.

I will outline what I believe you need to know to get started.

The purpose of this handbook is (1) to give you a working idea of the "terrain" of the counterfactual fiction genre known as alternate history, (2) help you familiarize yourself with its particular history and tropes, and (3) explain the basic how-to "rules" of counterfactual fiction construction. And I promise to use specific illustrations so you can *see* how it's done.

You can think of these rules, or conventions, as "tricks of the trade." They comprise a toolbox, if you will, for the craftsperson. And I've also included a Q & A chapter—a conversation of sorts with some of the most esteemed authors of counterfactual fiction— to show you how successful practitioners regard counterfactual fiction and their different "takes" on what *I* consider to be some of its foundation concepts. These writers include Harry Turtledove, Kim Stanley Robinson, Pamela Sargent, Lewis Shiner, Bruce Sterling, William Gibson, Lisa Goldstein, John Crowley, and Michael Swanwick, among many others. (And, lastly, for those of you who wish to pursue in depth some of the topics I touch on, I've also included the sources I consulted.)

So with all of the above notes and caveats in mind, let's open the toolbox—or, rather, take the toolbox out of the closet—and figure out what we're talking about.

##

2

Let's Examine What We're Talking about

And let's begin by taking a definitional stand!

Scholars and writers and critics have described fiction that hinges on a divergence from known history as "alternate history," "alternative history," "allohistory," "parahistory," "if-worlds," "counterfactuals," "uchronia," "uchronie," "alternate worlds" (or "alternative worlds").

I could probably come up with more, but, mercifully, won't.

To avoid confusion, I will call this special and unique form of fiction "counterfactual fiction." Although I'll readily admit that most writers I know refer to counterfactual stories and novels as "alternate history," the term alternate history can be misconstrued because it doesn't distinguish between counterfactual fiction and counterfactuals: the analytical thought experiments usually conducted by historians.

And then there is—of course!—a second definitional problem: what exactly do we mean by the term counterfactual fiction?

Counterfactual fiction is generally defined by its relation to history, and it comes into being through the writer's choice of a "divergence point," an alteration which creates a new branch of history that confounds or rejects the "real" history we think we know. A divergence point, or nexus point, as it is sometimes called, is an invented or inverted discrete historical event. You might also find these pivotal points described as jonbar hinges or jonbar points. The terms are derived from Jack Williamson's classic 1938 time travel story "The Legion of Time" about a war across time in which the fate of an alternate time stream and the future world of Jonbar "hinges" on whether a young boy named John Barr picks up a magnet or a pebble.

A writer may choose a divergence point that the reader can observe or give the reader enough information to assume a divergence point that has taken place in the story's "past." Either way, the consequences of divergence can range from a present shaped by the allies losing the Second World War ... or the South winning the American Civil War, to entirely altered worlds and modes of existence.

But whether a divergence point is observed or simply implied, all counterfactual fiction must in some way hinge on a divergence from known history, whether it be in the near or distant past. The genre critic Tom Shippey has suggested that a divergence point should be plausible, definite, small in itself, and massive in consequence (17).

I think this is a pretty good "rule."

However, when I questioned known practitioners of the craft, Pamela Sargent asked "What counts as a small change? The death of one person, any person, is a 'small' change in the world, given that we're all going to die, but it makes a difference whether that person is, say, a homeless man or President John F. Kennedy" (Dann, *Guide* 84).

Kim Stanley Robinson countered with a "reverse Shippey" big flow theory: "You need some very big changes to make any historical difference" (Dann, *Guide* 83).

And the Australian screenwriter and producer Mark Shirrefs turned the rule on its head by suggesting that a massive event can bring about a *small* consequence: "For example in the *War of the Worlds* movie with Tom Cruise, Martians invade the Earth, but unlike other stories where it's the defeat of the aliens that is the main narrative, here it's about the improvement of Tom's character's relationship with his family. So, a massive event—the invasion—causes a small consequence—a man gets on better with his kids" (Dann, *Guide* 81).

The differences of opinion here are emblematic or representative of the wildly divergent approaches writers can take to the craft of counterfactual fiction ... approaches which can all be valid in terms of conceptualization.

Bruce Sterling said, "I'm all for formulating concepts. They don't have to be correct to be genuinely useful to writers" (Dann, *Guide* 80).

This statement illustrates what may be an essential difference between a critical investigation and one that is practice-based. Thus, in order to provide workable conceptual tools for you, for those who wish to write counterfactual fiction, I will pick and choose from the "toolbox" of critical and practitioner-based "rules."

I suggest you do the same.

#

I mentioned earlier that it might be useful to know how the genre of counterfactual fiction came about. It certainly can't hurt to have an idea of how the genre came to be and its place in the literature of science fiction. But before we continue, let's agree (for now) on the following definition:

1   *Counterfactual fiction is basically a narrative in which an invented or inverted discrete historical event catalyzes a new and different sequence of subsequent events that changes the course of history as we know it.*

2   *A counterfactual fiction must, then, in some way hinge on a divergence from known history, whether it be in the near or the distant past.*

With that in mind, let's now move on to my admittedly potted history …

I'm not going to reach back to Livy and Herodotus, or to Disraeli's *Curiosities of Literature* (1824) entitled "Of a History of Events which Have Not Happened," or to Mark Twain's time-traveling *A Connecticut Yankee in King Arthur's Court* (1889) for possible examples of counterfactuals or counterfactual fictions. Modern counterfactual fiction is in fact a subgenre of science fiction; and we need to have some familiarity with the nature and some of the history of the larger "What-if" genre.

As with counterfactual fiction, even defining science fiction is a challenge. In 2010, the internet site *io9* asked "How Many definitions of science fiction are there" (Anders)? Although the author did not actually answer her titled question, she listed thirty-two definitions, from Damon Knight's "Science fiction is what we point to when we say it (Knight 1)" to Kingsley Amis's Science fiction is "that class of prose narrative treating of a situation that could not arise in the world we know, but which is hypothesised on the basis of some innovation in science or technology, or pseudo-science or pseudo-technology, whether human or extra-terrestrial in origin."

Quite a mouthful.

I would suggest we settle on Kim Stanley Robinson's excellent definition (or rather explanation) of science fiction because it embraces our topic at hand:

> Science Fiction is an historical literature. In fact this historicity defines the genre. The simplest way to say this is, "Science fiction stories are set in the future." Unpack this statement and we get something like the following: "In every SF narrative, there is an explicit or implicit fictional *history* that connects the period depicted to our present moment." The reader assumes that, starting from our present, a sequence of events will lead us to the "present" described in the narrative.
>
> Not all science fiction stories are set in the future. There are, for instance, the stories we call "alternative histories." But we can easily explain why the alternative history is part of SF, by revising the statement above to say, "In every SF narrative, there is an explicit or implicit fictional history that connects the period depicted to our present moment, or to some moment of our past." It is the same process, connecting to a different point in time. Because no SF story describes the actual future that will ensue in the real world, one could even say that all science fiction narratives are alternative histories— some branching away from our present, others branching away from some moment of our past (Robinson, "Notes" 54).

Although Wells and Verne are usually considered the "originators" of science fiction, it can arguably be claimed that the contemporary commercial *genre* of science fiction originated as an American phenomenon. It began in the 1920s with stories and serialized novels published in cheap 25 cent pulp magazines such as Hugo Gernsbach's *Amazing Stories*, which was the first magazine devoted exclusively to science fiction.

The science fiction pulp magazines might have been embarrassingly garish and the fiction often abominable; but it was the beginning of the commercial genre as we know it. Like-minded readers interacted with their favorite magazines via letter columns and with each other via mimeographed "fanzines," which later evolved into blogs and webzines on the World Wide Web. And some of these early readers/fans went on to become writers, the writers who would go on to create what's often referred to (usually with nostalgia … and sometimes with disgust!) as science fiction's "golden age" of the 1950s.

Writers read each other's stories and met each other at fan science fiction conventions; and certainly by the aforementioned 1950s, they were carrying on a healthy fiction "conversation" in magazines such as John W. Campbell's *Astounding/Analog* and Anthony Boucher's *The Magazine of Fantasy & Science Fiction* as writers reacted to each other's stories, influencing each other and creating the "furniture" of the genre … and a case could be made that it was this kind of larger ongoing "conversation" that later fueled new subgenres such as cyberpunk and steampunk.

Although steampunk—a "subgenre whose SF events take place against a nineteenth-century background" (Nicholls and Langford)—is itself a category of counterfactual fiction, it is interesting to note that counterfactual fiction has only recently (in relative terms) gained momentum as a *commercial* category by publishers. In fact, Matthew Schneider-Mayerson makes the claim that counterfactual fiction, which he calls the "literary counterfactual" was not recognized as a genre until the introduction of the Sidewise Award in 1995 (64).

I would argue that SF fans and writers considered counterfactual fiction to be a definite subgenre of SF before it became critically codified and commercially categorized in the 1990s. I certainly did in the late 1960s and 1970s when I was making my bones as a writer during a period of literary modernist and postmodernist experimentation in British and American SF called the New Wave. There was a substantial corpus of counterfactual fiction to draw upon; and I would have selectively pointed the reader to Murray Leinster's 1938 classic "Sidewise in Time," which introduced the concept to the genre (Stableford, Wolfe, and Langford); L. Sprague de Camp's *Lest Darkness Fall* (1941) and "Aristotle and the Gun" (1956); Ward Moore's novel of an undefeated American South, *Bring the Jubilee* (1953); Philip K. Dick's quintessential counterfactual fiction about an America under Japanese and Nazi rule: *The Man in the High Castle* (1962); Keith Robert's beautiful and elegiac depiction of the world after a victorious Spanish Armada: *Pavane* (1968); Vladimir Nabokov's mirror world of *Ada* (1969); Norman Spinrad's satiric *The Iron Dream* (1972), in which a German émigré named Hitler becomes a pulp SF illustrator and writer; *The*

Alteration by Kingsley Amis (1976), Brian Aldiss's *The Malachia Tapestry* (1977), an almost painterly depiction of a Renaissance city populated by the descendants of dinosaurs; and the bestselling detective novel *SS-GB* by Len Deighton (1978).

It was during this period—the 1960s and 1970s—that counterfactual fiction really began to flourish; it was also a period when science fiction was moving into the popular culture and starting to gain academic attention. It may well be, as Gavriel Rosenfeld asserts, that by the 1960s "the legitimization of science fiction as a widely accepted genre of creative expression helped boost the fortunes of its lesser-known allohistorical offshoot," that being alternate history ("Why" 92). And I also agree with Rosenfeld that "The rise of postmodernism, with its blurring of the boundaries between fact and fiction, its privileging of 'other' or alternate voices, and its playfully ironic reconfiguring of established historical verities, has encouraged the rise of counterfactual fiction" (92).

By the 1990s, "alternate history" was a definite commercial publishing category and other authors not associated with genre fiction began publishing novels that depicted different outcomes for the Second World War, a strong and enduring subject for counterfactual extrapolation: novels such as Robert Harris's bestselling *Fatherland* (1992), a detective story in the vein of Deighton's earlier *SSGB*; Newt Gingrich and William R. Forstchen's *1945* (1995); and Stephen Fry's *Making History* (1998), which posited an alternate timeline in which Hitler didn't exist. I might note, however, that like *SSGB*, these novels were published out of genre as "mainstream" novels.

To my mind, the two most important alternate history genre books of the 1990s were William Gibson and Bruce Sterling's *The Difference Engine* (1990), a brilliant extrapolation of a Victorian computer age, and Harry Turtledove's now classic example of alternate history—*The Guns of the South* (1992)—a breakout novel in which the outcome of the Civil War (another popular subject for counterfactual fiction) is reversed by AK-47s sent back in time from our century.

A perusal of Robert B. Schmunk's *Uchronia: The Alternate History List*, which brands itself as "a bibliography of over 3,200 novels, stories, essays and other printed material involving the 'what ifs' of history" ("Welcome") and his *Sidewise Awards for Alternate History* page ("Sidewise") will give the interested reader a good indication of the state of the genre in terms of books being published and those judged to be of merit.

There were/are so many that I will only point somewhat randomly at a few books that have gained top-of-mind awareness: Kim Stanley Robinson's *The Years of Rice and Salt* (2002), a postmodern counterfactual *tour de force* about the repercussions of the Black Death (in which Europeans die out); Philip Roth's *The Plot Against America* (2004), a counterfactual timeline in which Lindbergh becomes president of the United States and forms a pact with the Nazis, a major novel which rests uneasily with the reader's (or rather this reader's) suspension of disbelief; Michael Chabon's *The Yiddish Policeman's Union* (2007), a detective story set in an alternate Alaska; *11/22/63* (2011), Stephen King's time travel novel about an attempt to prevent the Kennedy assassination; Nisi Shawl's steampunk utopia *Everfair* (2016) which chronicles an alternate Africa that develops steam power before the European colonialists; and Mary Robinette Kowal's multi-award-winning novel *The Calculating Stars* (2018) in which America wins the space race in 1952.

I would also include such thought-provoking works as Phong Nguyen's *Pages from the Textbook of Alternate History* (2014), which scrutinizes Thomas Carlyle's "great man theory" and plays with the idea of history as story. And there are many compelling counterfactual explorations of gender, culture, and identity, such as Shelley Parker-Chan's novel *She Who Became the Sun* (2022), which she describes as "a queer re-imagining of the rise to power of the founding emperor of the Ming dynasty" (墨客, hunxi. "Rewriting"); Lavie Tidhar's *Unholy Land* (2018), which depicts a modern Jewish State called Palestina in sub-Saharan Africa; Annalee Newitz's feminist novel *The Future of Another Timeline* (2019), which examines time travel and competing theories of history; Janeen Webb and Andrew Enstice's *The Five Star Republic* (2021), an historically plausible vision of a solar-powered nineteenth-century Australia; and Laurent Binet's *Civilizations* (2021), which depicts a counterfactual timeline in which the Incas colonize Spain.

To move on and complete this introductory overview, we should note some of the subgenres associated with counterfactual fiction, which include secret history, historical fantasy, time travel, and parallel worlds.

Secret History: Gordon B. Chamberlain distinguishes counterfactual fiction, which he refers to as "what might have been" from secret history, which he wryly (and accurately) describes as "what might have been if only we knew" (282). Basically, secret history is fiction about an event that has no effect or is not noticeable in our consensual historical timeline. In my novel *The Memory Cathedral: a Secret History of Leonardo da Vinci*, I took advantage of a gap in the record of Leonardo's life to enable him to become a munitions engineer for the Devatdar of Syria and build the inventions he had only drawn in his notebooks: flying machines, submarines, Gatling guns, scuba gear, parachutes, etc. I based this idea on the possibility that he did in actual fact visit the Middle East, and then I invented an unrecorded tribal war.

But none of Leonardo's actions changed or affected the timeline that led to our present. It is history as it might have been if we only knew. I also utilized this material to create a novelette called "Da Vinci Rising" in which it is evident that Leonardo's flying machines *will* cause a break with history as we know it. Thus, the novel is secret history, the novelette counterfactual fiction.

Historical Fantasy: As John Birmingham has said, "If you don't have a divergence point, even one that exists only off the page and in the author's private knowledge, then you don't have alternate history. You have fantasy" (Dann, *Guide* 58). However, historical fantasy, as it relates to counterfactual fiction, might be considered an umbrella term to classify those stories that *appear* to be counterfactual fiction, but don't provide definite reasons for the divergence (Alkon 68). These are stories that don't require the reader to be familiar with historical incidents. Some scholars would also claim that if a story employs "mild forms of magic and other elements of difference to engage the reader" it is a historical fantasy rather than counterfactual fiction (Ransom 274).

I would disagree with this and would point out that Keith Robert's *Pavane*, a foundation work in the alternate history genre, does indeed employ mild forms of magic. Other scholars would categorize a counterfactual fiction as historical fantasy if it *feels* like fantasy (Ransom 274). I would disagree with this also. But I *would* agree with Richard Harland when he says that "genre shouldn't be an exclusive either-or way to categorize fiction" (Dann, *Guide* 79).

Time Travel: For a clear definition of this science fiction subgenre, I would choose this one from the *Alternate History Wiki*:

Time travel involves traveling backward, or forward, in time. A time travel story is an alternate history if the time travel in question causes a change in the past, and that change is shown leading to a significantly different world. *A lot of time travel stories are alternate histories in a trivial sense in that the consequences of changing the past are briefly shown or mentioned, but the story deals primarily with the time travelling itself* [italics mine]. Many other time travel stories involve time travel that all takes place in our future, or time travel to the past which does not lead to a world whose history departs substantially from that of our own. Time travel stories are thus not necessarily alternate history, although there is a fair amount of common ground between the two genres.

(Jason777)

Parallel Worlds: According to Brian Stableford and David Langford, "A parallel world is another universe situated 'alongside' our own, displaced from it along a spatial fourth dimension (parallel worlds are often referred to in SF as 'other dimensions'). Although whole universes may lie parallel in this sense, most stories focus on parallel Earths. The parallelworld idea forms a useful framework for the notion of alternate history, and is often used in this way" ("Parallel").

I agree with Stableford and Langford, but I have included parallel worlds in this listing only because there are conflicting interpretations of the category, such as this more limiting one from the previously referenced *Alternate History Wiki*:

Parallel worlds are worlds which have never been the same as our own, just as parallel lines are lines which never meet. In order for a world to have an alternate history relative to our own, its history had to be the same up until a point where it diverged from our own, thus leading its history down a different path. The term 'parallel worlds', in contrast, is properly applied to worlds which have always been different from our own. They may be similar in many ways, but they have never been exactly the same. Typically, parallel worlds are differentiated by differences in the laws of physics (especially by the presence of magic). Such worlds are by definition not alternate histories.

(Jason777)

My earnest suggestion would be to treat all definitions and categories regarding science fiction—and by definition(!) counterfactual fiction—as permeable (and tentative).

#

It might be useful at this point to create a provisional "model" of counterfactual fiction, which might give you a better understanding of the form and historical placement of any given work you encounter. Why would you need such a thing? Well, one of the very best ways to learn craft and technique is to analyze how others do it. And, yes, the bit that follows is theoretical and critical. I suggest you plough through it anyway.

I should also emphasize that this analysis is only one of *many* possible ways to view the genre ... my way, so, as with many pronouncements about the craft of fiction, you might want to keep the container of grains of salt close by. With that in mind, let us recklessly continue to mix metaphors and cut out a model of counterfactual fiction from the cloth of Karen Hellekson, Corinne Buckland, Richard Ned Lebow, Edgar Chapman, and author and critic Joanna Russ.

Karen Hellekson is one of the foremost scholars of counterfactual fiction. In her invaluable study *The Alternate History: Refiguring Historical Time*, she has created a valuable taxonomy by dividing counterfactual fiction into categories according to the author's selection of a divergence point or break from consensual history. These categories include (1) the nexus story, (2) the true alternate history, and (3) the parallel worlds story. She writes: "Nexus stories occur at the moment of the break. The true alternate history occurs after the break, sometimes a long time after. And the parallel worlds story implies that there was no break—that all events that could have occurred did occur" (5).

According to this taxonomy, Harry Turtledove's *The Guns of the South* would be characterized as a "nexus story," as would my novel *The Rebel* in which our consensual timeline bifurcates when James Dean survives his accident on Highway 466 in his Spyder Porche. (Advance warning: I often will refer to my own work to analyze and explain story and intention from an authorial perspective.)

A classic example of a "true alternate history story" would be Philip K. Dick's *The Man in the High Castle*, which takes place in a timeline long after the Axis powers have won the Second World War.

An example of "the parallel worlds story" would be Murray Leinster's short story about crossing multiple timelines, "Sidewise in Time" or Philip Jose Farmer's lovely conceit "Sail On! Sail On," a story that describes a voyage by Columbus in a universe where there are no Americas and the world is … flat.

There are also many stories such as Ward Moore's *Bring the Jubilee* that combine categories. *Bring the Jubilee* is a "nexus story," as it focuses on a time-traveling protagonist: a historian who returns to the scene of the Battle of Gettysburg and inadvertently changes the outcome of the Civil War. But as the time traveler is from another timeline, it can also be considered a "parallel worlds story" since in the traveler's timeline the South won the Civil War.

And a closer look at *The Man in the High Castle* will reveal that it is also a parallel worlds story, as well as a "true alternate history story." These categories are quite porous, and any given story may well fit comfortably into more than one category.

Lastly, I believe an additional category is needed to complete what we might consider to be the topographical component of our model; and I've conflated the critical ideas of Richard Ned Lebow's "miracle world counterfactuals" and Corinne Buckland's "transcendent history" into a new category I call "the transcendent counterfactual story." Although some might consider this category contentious because it edges onto the border of fantasy, I see it as a useful mechanism to allow consideration of those works that translate tropes of myth and magic into a counterfactual framework.

Unlike Hellekson's three categories, the transcendent counterfactual story is not defined by its reliance on the placement (or existence) of a divergence point, but on its relationship to a plausible or possible metaphysical perspective.

Thus Buckland claims that "instead of asking 'what if?' to show a sequence of changed consequences in an altered world, [transcendent history] envisions history from a God's or gods'-eye perspective and juxtaposes the experience of individuals against a panoramic, eternal view" (80). She proposes and represents transcendent history as a new genre exemplified by the holocaust novel *The Book Thief* (2007) by Markus Zusak, which she suggests could also be considered alternate history (74). She argues that a new genre is required "to accommodate the strength of Zusak's achievement" (78). Whatever the validity of the case Buckland makes for Zusak and transcendent history as a separate genre, I will consider transcendent history to be a category of counterfactual fiction, as I believe it fills a necessary gap in our definition.

Lebow takes a different perspective, but is targeting the same counterfactual category, if you like. He distinguishes between miracle world counterfactuals and "plausible world counterfactuals," which "are intended to impress readers as realistic; they cannot violate our understanding of what was technologically, culturally, temporally, or otherwise possible" (160). He considers plausible world counterfactuals "historical near misses" (161). Miracle world counterfactuals, on the other hand, "violate our understanding of what is plausible" and may "help us work though moral and scholarly problems" (161). According to Lebow, "The utility of miracle counterfactuals does not depend on their realism, but on the analytical utility of considering alternative worlds" (162).

My 2020 novel *Shadows in the Stone* is an example of a transcendent counterfactual. It tests the generally agreed upon boundaries of counterfactual fiction by creating a completely divergent ontology, a "possible world" in which the objects of religious belief are real and perceivable and their actions consequential. It re-imagines an Italian Renaissance that is permeated by Gnostic doctrines rather than the familiar culture and religion derived by the decisions of the Council of Nicea and extrapolates an entire system of myth and belief presented through the points of view of characters who have a bicameral mindset, a different form of consciousness which "allows" them to see and hear the projections of their belief.

I would direct the reader to consider whether a fantasy novel in which an alternate historical timeline is a vital, overarching, and integral element might be categorized as a transcendent counterfactual. And I would point to work such as P. Djèlí Clark's first novel *A Master of Djinn* (2021), which depicts an alternate Cairo where myth, magic, and technology have equivalent values.

The transcendent counterfactual category can also serve to clarify and focus counterfactual novels that only contain *elements* of myth and magic, such as Pamela Sargent's carefully researched *Climb the Wind* (1999), which speculates on how native American tribes might have united after the Civil War to defeat the US Army and prevent US expansion. Sargent writes:

> I might have pushed the boundaries a bit in my novel *Climb the Wind*, which was inspired by a comment Louis L'Amour

(one of my father's favorite writers, as he was a fan of Westerns) made during an interview: "The history of the United States would have been very different if there had been an Indian Genghis Khan." A number of my characters, both real historical figures and invented characters, have visions, as some of them (Crazy Horse) did in real life. (Visions were an important part of Plains Indian culture.) In these visions, some of them see what happened to them or those near them in our world, as opposed to their world. That might seem to make this novel more of a magic realist or historical fantasy work than alternate history. But something was telling me that leaving out any role for visions wouldn't be true to some of the cultures I was depicting, and the visions also served as a commentary on alternative time lines.

(Dann, Guide 110)

Thus, Sargent introduces elements of the implausible or miracle transcendent—that is, magic and visions—into a realistically conceived and constructed counterfactual fiction in order to *strengthen* the authenticity of the story world by including the "worldview" of the characters living within the culture.

Before we leave this topic, I should also mention that there is a narrow yet very interesting subgenre of fantasy that could be characterized as transcendent counterfactual fiction. What might be termed "literary alternate history" refers to those stories and novels that extrapolate imaginary worlds out of the historically popular imaginary worlds created by authors such as Jane Austen, Bram Stoker, and Mary Shelley. Kim Newman's *Anno Dracula* series (1993–2015), in which Count Dracula conquers Great Britain, and John Kessel's *Pride and Prometheus* (2018), which is an amalgamation of Jane Austen's *Pride and Prejudice*, and Mary Shelley's *Frankenstein* are examples of this refractive subgenre.

#

As well as the categories described that divide counterfactual fiction according to the author's selection of a divergence point, we can also categorize any given work by determining what "model" of history informs it.

Karen Hellekson brilliantly applied Hayden White's four models of history to categorize counterfactual fiction in terms of "beginning and end, design and disorder" (*Alternate* 2):

The eschatological model of history is concerned with final events or an ultimate destiny, be it the ultimate destiny of humankind or of history. Its opposite is genetic history, or history concerned with origin, development, or cause. The entropic model of history assumes that the process of history is one of disorder or randomness. Its opposite is teleological or future-oriented history, history that seems to have a design or purpose. Though the alternate history may focus on any of these four models, as a genre, the alternate history fundamentally concerns itself with the genesis of history.

(*Alternate* 2)

And we can also break down genre alternate history into eras. Edgar L. Chapman does just this, which can be summarized as (i) *The early years from 1926 to 1945*, characterized by counterfactual fiction treated experimentally and playfully as a novelty device to exploit adventure, humor, and "mildly speculative thought," (ii) *The post-Second World War era from 1945 to 1968*, characterized by ambitious narrative exploration of the possibilities of the genre, seminal works of influence, and serious cautionary tales; and (iii) *The post-modern era from 1969 to the present*, a time when counterfactual fiction becomes fictional technique and is characterized by explorations of problematic political, moral, and cultural issues (and I would add—and emphasize—contemporary gender and racial issues); deliberate and ironic displays of multiple time streams; and portrayals of historical contingency, indeterminacy, and other post-modern concerns (9–16).

Although one can find counterfactual fiction in one era that embodies the characteristics of other eras, I've found this outline to be useful as a rough guideline, especially if coupled with author and critic Joanna Russ's three stages of science fiction described in her seminal essay "The Wearing Out of Genre Materials."

Russ calls her first stage in the evolution of a genre construct "Innocence" because "the progress of the story is merely that of drawing close and closer to a marvel and the story's climax consists in a brief glimpse of the marvel, rather like pulling a rabbit out of a hat" ("Wearing" 48). In the second stage, "Plausibility," the essential science fiction question "What if … ?" is being asked, and the treatment of the story "becomes complicated, plausible and … realistic" (49). When a genre construct reaches the third stage, which Russ calls "Decadence," it may become frozen into ritual like Westerns, become stylized, or once-important genre devices may become metaphorical elements employed for other purposes. In any case, the explanatory interest, so important to second stage stories, is missing (50). This would fit with Chapman's post-modern third stage, and could be used to describe the state of steampunk, which "appears as a designation for everything from the Western-flavored space opera *Firefly* (2005) to pseudo-Edwardian colonialist high adventure anime ... to the alternative fashion of mock-Victorian clothing" (Nevins 513).

So, let's see how this works by applying the topographical/ longitudinal model to Keith Roberts's *Pavane*. Robert's novel diverges from our historical timeline when Queen Elizabeth is assassinated and, as a result, England is defeated by the Spanish Armada and the Catholic Church becomes the most powerful institution in Europe and the New World.

As this novel takes place long after the occurrence of the divergence point (Elizabeth's assassination), we could categorize it as a "true alternate history story." (And as there are "mild forms" of magic present in the novel, it could also be analyzed as a transcendent counterfactual.)

We can also classify it as genetic history, as it is "concerned with origin, development, or cause" (Hellekson, *Alternate* 2); and since it doesn't use an explanatory trope/device such as a time machine but presents the altered history realistically as a given, it could be classified it as a second stage genre construct, á la Russ. It also fits easily into Chapman's second stage, as it is certainly an ambitious narrative exploration and a seminal work of influence.

Applying the model to an experimental counterfactual fiction, such as my own novel *Shadows in the Stone*, a work which might otherwise be difficult to categorize as counterfactual fiction, might be instructive. Because the novel occurs after (what must be assumed as) a series of small and barely discernible divergence points over a period of time to form a counterfactual renaissance Italy influenced by a combination of Gnostic beliefs and classicism, it *could* be categorized as a "true alternate history story." But this novel does not depict a specific divergence point or series of divergence points where the timeline in which the events of the story are represented breaks off (i.e. branches away) from our own consensual timeline. In this respect, it bears a kinship with Brian Aldiss's counterfactual parallel worlds renaissance novel *The Malacia Tapestry* (1977) in which the Malacians' "ancestral descent" is *claimed* to be from dinosaurs rather than apes.

Shadows in the Stone could also be categorized as eschatological because it is concerned with the ultimate destiny of humankind and history itself (Hellekson, *Alternate* 2) and also as a parallel worlds story (5) because the protagonist Louisa passes from one alternate universe/timeline to another through a "crack in the sky."

Although a counterfactual story might fit into more than one category, I would concentrate on the counterfactual category that best captures its overarching character. I think *Shadows* is a transcendent counterfactual because its defining element is a vision of history from the dual perspectives of men and angels interacting with each other along the span of eternity according to Gnostic and biblical canons and beliefs. "It envisions history from a God's or gods'-eye perspective and juxtaposes the experience of individuals against a panoramic, eternal view" (Buckland 80). It is, as Lebow indicates, a counterfactual fiction that violates our modern, secular understanding of what is plausible (61).

As *Shadows* could be considered ambitious and experimental both in conception and narration, it would comfortably fit into Chapman's second stage (9); and as the treatment of the story is "complicated, plausible, and … realistic," it could fit into Russ's second stage ("Wearing" 49). However, I would place it somewhere between Russ's first and second stage constructs because it employs a "marvel": the "crack in the sky": I should note that Russ treats the term "marvel" in a slightly different sense than I do. She uses the term to refer to the novelty glimpsed at the climax of a story categorized as a first stage "innocent" genre construct, whereas I am enlarging its meaning to reference the use of marvels such as time-machines, my "crack in the sky," or devices such as Stephen King's time-stairs (*11/2/63: a Novel* [2011]) in stories that could be categorized as second stage genre constructs ("Wearing" 48–9).

And I think that's probably enough backgrounding … enough about definitions, genre history, and analytical model-making! It's time to figure out what we're actually doing when we (try to) write counterfactual fiction … and then figure out how to do it right.

3

Thinking about History and Your Readers

When we write a counterfactual fiction, when we set our proverbial pens to paper or type those ghostly words with a keyboard, we are theorizing about history and morality and choice ... and we are taking a definite position about the nature of history and morality and choice.

That's a *big* sentence, but the very idea of alternate history is about exploring choice: we choose divergence points that allow us to explore different outcomes initiated by different choices, chance, or slightly changed events that can shift our characters into different situational presents or pasts than our own. We make those choices (although, at least in my experience as a creator, it sometimes feels as if the *characters* are doing the choosing). But the kinds of choices we impart to our characters and the nature of the forces we create to drive their actions in our counterfactual story worlds also reflect a particular position on the nature of history itself.

Nor do we necessarily have to be aware that we are assuming or advocating a theory of history. When I was writing my novel *The Rebel* and the related stories which are collected in *Promised Land*, I was not consciously advocating any particular theory such as (what might be considered as the most obvious) some variation of Thomas Carlyle's "great man theory," which Carlyle described as "the history of what man has accomplished in this world ... the history of Great Men who have worked here." Carlyle wrote:

> They were the leaders of men, these great ones; the modelers, patterns, and in a wide sense creators of whatsoever the general

mass of men contrived to do or attain; all things that we see standing accomplished in the world are properly the outer material result, the practical realization and embodiment, of Thoughts that dwelt in the Great Men sent into the world: the soul of the whole world's history, it may justly be considered, were the history of these."

(Lecture 1, par 1)

Or as the critic and novelist Phong Nguyen put it: "any characterization of human history that implies that the progress of civilization comes about exclusively through the forceful actions of unprecedented visionaries" (3).

But in his introduction to my collection *Promised Land*, Kim Stanley Robinson suggested that I was doing quite the opposite:

> Though at first it may seem so, more or less by definition, I think the content of the stories themselves indicates Dann does not believe in the great man theory. Most of his famous characters are trapped in their roles, and the background history that unfolds in the narrative is very similar to what happened in our own remembered history, no matter what they do. In that sense this collection functions more like a secret history than an alternative history, explaining as it does some hidden parts of what happened in the Fifties and Sixties, but keeping the overall movement of history the same. There is the suggestion in *The Rebel* that if James Dean had lived he might have served as a rallying point for progressive forces in American politics, in the same manner that Ronald Reagan served as a rallying point for the reactionary forces that eventually won power in our Eighties. But as the events of Dann's narrative play out, it becomes clear that his celebrity protagonists do not manage to make much of a difference in the course of events. As one story puts it, whether James Dean or Paul Newman got the main role in *The Hustler*, American political life would proceed much the same; and even when James Dean does get elected governor of California, he does little differently from his predecessor Pat Brown, before fate takes him in a different direction entirely. Even the most powerful individuals are hooped by necessity, these stories seem to say; so that the ultimate historical statement embodied in them

seems to come down firmly against the great man theory, and for something that might be characterized as a chaotic and inexorable tumult of collective human actions, with a large and permanent element of tragedy and wasted potential.

(xi–xii)

I would venture a guess that some few writers such as myself often discover and/or clarify, whether as conscious or unconscious process, what they believe regarding ethics, morality, causality, determinism, the nature of history, etc. through the very process of research and writing.

Writing is, or can be, a process of self-discovery.

For me, counterfactual fiction and fiction in general is a means of analyzing my beliefs and ideas, even when I'm writing novels such as *Shadows*, which involve belief systems I would never consider to be "true." But, as Robinson also pointed out, I am interested in a sort of "archeology" of myth and culture and the interface between them. He writes, and I believe he is correct, that I am engaged (at least in *The Rebel* and my collection *Promised Land*) in a "different kind of 'what if' than that presented in the usual alternative history: not only 'what if James Dean had lived?' but also, and perhaps more importantly ... what if most of the myths we tell about that generation of celebrities were based on truths?" ("Introduction" viii–ix):

This is another kind of fictional idea generator, a kind of archeology of narrative, which says: If the myths and rumors about these people were based on real events, refracted through the lens of retellings, what would have had to have happened, back at the beginning, in order to create the material for us to spin out those myths and rumors? Regarding only the various clouds and columns of smoke, can one then present to the reader the fire itself?

(viii–ix)

The "truth," if that is the appropriate word, of my beliefs, yearnings, desires, and perceptions of the workings of the world often lies in the allegorical or metaphorical "understructure" of my work and in the interaction between my characters and their world(s). And I often discover what I think about a particular moral, ethical, historical, or even personal issue *after* I've "watched" my characters bring them to life. Other counterfactual fiction writers craft their work as conscious explorations of specific theories or issues. But whether or not *you* consciously address, implicitly or explicitly, one or another of the theories of history and moral choice (Kessel, "Remaking History" 85), your story is nevertheless an argument about the workings of history.

Robinson suggests that the author's choice of a divergence point "will tend to define at least part of the writer's theory of history; was it great man stuff? Or a 'for loss of a nail the shoe was lost' etc. type theory, maybe out of chaos theory? and so on" (Dann, *Guide* 63).

And a given work of counterfactual fiction may also indicate or illustrate the author's own model(s) of history. To quote Robinson again: "I was very aware that my alternative history stories were being written to illustrate the changed historical path I was introducing with the story. I was aware I was proposing also a kind of theory as to how history is made by people" (Dann, *Guide* 69).

Whatever your implied or explicit theory of history—whether conscious or unconscious, whether prescriptive or descriptive—the reader of science fiction, historical fiction, fantasy, and historical fantasy doesn't necessarily need to be familiar with the history surrounding the story being told.

A science fiction story might take place in a far future in which the differences from our world, our present, are revealed within the story; or if the story takes place in the near future, the author can assume the reader is at least somewhat familiar with the present state of the world. And although fantasy, specifically high fantasy, often employs tropes generally familiar to the reader such as medieval settings, Arthurian references, European myths and legends, etc., familiarity with a specific historical time is not required. (Of course, it goes without saying that in the case of historical fiction and historical fantasy, the reader who is familiar with the historical period will be able to read, understand, and gain pleasure on a much deeper, critical level than the unfamiliar reader. And a case might be made that the same argument could be claimed for any given secret history, depending, of course, on how fantastical and believable the premise.)

Nor is historical familiarity required to read, comprehend, and enjoy a historical fantasy—or for that matter a straight historical novel. In the latter, the reader's enjoyment may well be in the delight (or illusion) of learning about what really happened or could have happened in a previous time. I would suggest that all of these genres and subgenres—counterfactual fiction included—involve to some degree or another what Darko Suvin refers to as "cognitive estrangement" (the experience of encountering and understanding a world estranged from our own) and also, perhaps, the discovery of the "novum," which author and critic Damien Broderick describes as "an intrusive novelty so strange, and at first inexplicable, that it deserves a category of its own ... " ("Novum").

But the reader of traditional counterfactual fiction *is* required to be familiar with the consensual history leading up to and/or subsequent to the story being told because counterfactual fiction is *defined* by its relation to history, and it comes into being through the practitioner's choice of a divergence point: that defining Jonbar hinge.

This certainly limits the readership for the genre, although as we've seen, there is a devoted and enthusiastic audience for counterfactual fiction, and the widespread familiarity of readers with the American Civil War and the Second World War probably accounts for the popularity of stories and novels that depict counterfactual alternatives to these momentous events. As Gavriel D. Rosenfeld has said: "On the whole, alternate history as a genre tends to focus on pivotal events of world historical importance that have squarely left their mark on the world of today. These events, or 'points of divergence,' include the death of kings and politicians, decisive military victories or defeats, the rise of grand cultural or religious movements, and even demographic trends, such as migrations or plagues" (*World* 11).

There are, of course, many exceptions to Rosenfeld's observation; and some of those exceptions can make for very interesting reading indeed: I would direct the reader to authors such as Howard Waldrop, whose wry and ironic stories such as "Ike at the Mike" (1982) have gained him a devoted readership.

Remember Shippey's rule, mentioned earlier, that counterfactual fiction "should be (1) plausible, (2) definite, (3) small in itself, and (4) massive in consequence" (17)? Well, Michael Swanwick writes (with both accuracy and Waldrop's abovementioned wryness) that "There are no rules. Or, rather, there used to be rules before Howard Waldrop wrote 'Ike at the Mike,' in which hearing a snatch of live music causes the young Dwight D. Eisenhower to abandon his plans for a military career in order to become a jazz musician. This is implausible to an extreme. You could argue that by Shippey's rule 'Ike at the Mike' is not a good alternate history story. Yet it's a good story, it's alternate history, and without invoking the rule there's no way of denying that it's a good alternate history story" (Dann, *Guide* 85). Although I agree with Swanwick, I note for the record John Kessel had a very different reaction: "This story has always bothered me. As far as I know, Elvis had little interest in or capacity for politics, and Eisenhower had absolutely no musical ability. The story trades on the novelty of imagining these people in what seem to us very surprising careers, but it is in my opinion completely bogus ... It's a conceit, almost a joke, not an illumination" (Dann, *Guide* 86).

What can we take away from this?

Perhaps it is that the success of any counterfactual fiction depends on the level of virtuosity that the writer can bring to the craft. And a high level of virtuosity can also allow the practitioner to *break* the rules. Need I state that in order to successfully break the rules, you need to know the rules ... and the problems you are likely to encounter.

Such as how do you deal with reader familiarity?

In order for any counterfactual fiction to make sense, to be comprehensible, it requires a reader with at least a passing knowledge of the actual history your alternate timeline is referencing. But what if you're writing about a little-known historical period? What if most of your hypothetical readers don't have a clue about the actual history you are referencing?

Accommodating the readers' unfamiliarity with particular cultures and historical events is a major problem for all of us who try to write the gnarly, offbeat, and perhaps cutting-edge counterfactual stories that allow us to "glimpse through their thickets some signs of what is truly happening to us in the unfoldings of time" (Zebrowski in Dann, *Guide* 117). Paul Alkon was, unfortunately, correct when he wrote:

> For postmodern (or other) readers among whom ignorance of history and indifference to it is the norm, alternate history will often seem incomprehensible because crucial points of divergence from the past may not even be noticed. Consequently

it will be unattractive by comparison with more self-contained fantasies of future, parallel, or simply different worlds, or with fiction set in the reader's own time and place (69).

Thus Mary Rosenblum, who looks for divergence points "that open up a wealth of possibilities, both social and historical, and that can be explored on multiple levels" (Dann, *Guide* 103), also comments that "a divergence point needs to effect a change that even the average reader with today's minimal grasp of history can recognize" (20). And in a column written for *Tor.com* entitled "Challenges of Writing Alternate History Set in Other Cultures," Ekaterina Sedia wrote that because of the unfamiliar setting of her counterfactual novel *Heart of Iron*, "many readers and reviewers weren't sure where, exactly, the history had been altered" (par 3).

The novel was set in a nineteenth-century counterfactual Russia in which the Decembrist movement was successful.

She went on to explain that "unlike a novel set in a secondary (imaginary) world, there is no useful way of working this information into the book: alternate history explicitly relies on readers' pre-existing knowledge. There's simply no place to say 'well, in the real world, the Decembrists lost, and the Crimean War actually took place without Chinese involvement.' This information has to be extraneous to the story and thus there is no way to ensure that the reader will receive this information" ("Challenges," par 4–5).

Although I agree that an easily recognizable divergence point makes the task of creating an alternate history *significantly* easier, there are a number of techniques available to overcome reader unfamiliarity. Sedia offers a few suggestions, such as relying on readers to find the necessary information themselves, offering supplementary material on a website, and providing an appendix or a bibliography in the book itself. She does admit that these suggestions are less than ideal ("Challenges," par 6–8). With the exception of ancillary material provided in the book, that is, her idea of an appendix, which we will discuss further on, I would not consider those suggestions to be particularly effective or useful.

It's up to the writer to bring the reader up to speed through the text itself.

I don't believe we can rely on a casual reader to look elsewhere … nor should we! It is the job of the writer to guide the reader. I would agree with Michael Swanwick, a respected and fabulously inventive writer, who notes the importance of:

> An awareness of what history the reader might reasonably be expected to know. If a story hinges on George Washington becoming a British general, that fact would not need much exposition. If its Jonbar point is that Nicola Tesla stayed with Edison's laboratory rather than defecting to George Westinghouse, *a great deal more work will be required to make it clear that this did not happen in our own history and why it is a significant enough moment to radically change history* (italics mine).
>
> (Dann, *Guide* 78)

One of the joys of reading counterfactual fiction is the visceral and intellectual thrill of discovering the rippling consequences, the branchings both small and massive that emanate from the divergence point. I agree with Michael Chabon that the "aftermath" of the divergence point is more interesting than the divergence point itself (qtd. in Anders, "10 Worst," par 9).

Or as the critic Edward James wrote: "Much of the pleasure derived from reading these works lies in determining where the Jonbar point lies, and in enjoying the way in which the author has worked out the fictional world, and in some cases, dealt with the characters that the alternative world shares with ours" (114).

However surprising the divergence point, it is the reader's consequent encounters with the logically ensuing "novums"— the charged, disorienting recognition and comprehension of each deviation from our own fragile consensual history—that provide the most exciting and illuminating perspectives. And I would suggest that these particular perspectives, which further catalyze a unique fusion of emotion and intellect, cannot be found in contemporary realistic fiction or for that matter, nonfiction. As the historian Niall Ferguson writes, "To understand how it actually was, we therefore need to understand how it actually wasn't—but how, to contemporaries it might have been" (87).

So, then, how do we bring the reader up to speed when the period of history we want to write about might be unfamiliar and the Jonbar point not readily apparent? To begin, let us investigate Michael Swanwick's earlier point about more work being required to write about someone such as Nicola Tesla as opposed to a popularly known historical figure such as George Washington.

Lewis Shiner has in fact written a short, brilliantly jolting counterfactual fiction story entitled "White City" about one of Tesla's actual ideas: "the 'Terrestrial Night Light,' a plan to electrically charge the ionosphere so that the earth would be illuminated 24 hours a day." (Dann, *Guide* 110).

In "White City," which is only 2,100 words long, Shiner is able to give the unfamiliar reader enough information to place the story in a comprehensible historical context and then locate the divergence point, enabling the reader to have a visceral "sense" of both the "real" and the alternative histories and thus to experience/comprehend the logically ensuing novums. And Shiner does this without having to resort to information dumps or asking the reader to access supplemental material.

For reasons that I trust will soon become apparent, I must respectfully disagree with Ekaterina Sedia's contention quoted earlier that "There's simply no *place* [italics mine] to say 'well, in the real world, the Decembrists lost, and the Crimean War actually took place without Chinese involvement'" ("Challenges," par 4–5). There is indeed a place, and it is located within the story. Certainly there are *degrees* of difficulty—and I will endeavor to examine the far ends of that particular bell-shaped curve in a few moments—but it might be instructive to deconstruct Shiner's story first to appreciate how some of these difficulties can be overcome.

So, at this point, I invite you to take a break from me and read Lewis Shiner's brilliant story, which follows. Enjoy!

##

4

Taking a Break from Me

"White City" by Lewis Shiner

Tesla lifts the piece of sirloin to his lips. Its volume is approximately .25 cubic inches, or .02777 of the entire steak. As he chews, he notices a water spot on the back of his fork. He takes a fresh napkin from the stack at his left elbow and scrubs the fork vigorously.

He is sitting at a private table in the refreshment stand at the west end of the Court of Honor. He looks out onto the Chicago World's Fair and Columbian Exposition. It is October of 1893. The sun is long gone and the reflections of Tesla's electric lights sparkle on the surface of the Main Basin, turning the spray from the fountain into glittering jewels. At the far end of the Basin stands the olive-wreathed Statue of the Republic in flowing robes. On all sides the White City lies in pristine elegance, testimony to the glorious architecture of ancient Greece and Rome. Its chilly streets are populated by mustached men in topcoats and sturdy women in woolen shawls.

The time is 9:45. At midnight, Nikola Tesla will produce his greatest miracle. The number twelve seems auspicious. It is important to him, for reasons he cannot understand, that it is divisible by three.

Anne Morgan, daughter of financier J. Pierpoint Morgan, stands at a little distance from his table. Though still in finishing school she is tall, self-possessed, strikingly attractive. She is reluctant to disturb Tesla, knowing he prefers to dine alone. Still she is drawn to him irresistibly. He is rake thin and handsome as the devil himself, with steel gray eyes that pierce through to her soul.

"Mr. Tesla," she says, "I pray I am not disturbing you."

Tesla looks up, smiles gently. "Miss Morgan." He begins to rise.

"Please, do not get up. I was merely afraid I would miss you. I had hoped we might walk together after you finished here."

"I would be delighted."

"I shall await you there, by the Basin."

She withdraws. Trailing a gloved hand along the balustrade, she tries to avoid the drunken crowds which swarm the Exposition Grounds. Tomorrow the Fair will close and pass into history. Already there are arguments as to what is to become of these splendid buildings. There is neither money to maintain them nor desire to demolish them. Chicago's Mayor, Carter Harrison, worries that they will end up filthy and vandalized, providing shelter for the hundreds of poor who will no longer have jobs when the Fair ends.

Her thoughts turn back to Tesla. She finds herself inordinately taken with him. At least part of the attraction is the mystery of his personal life. At age thirty-seven he has never married nor been engaged. She has heard rumors that his tastes might be, to put it delicately, Greek in nature. There is no evidence to support this gossip and she does not credit it. Rather it seems likely that no one has yet been willing to indulge the inventor's many idiosyncrasies.

She absently touches her bare left ear lobe. She no longer wears the pearl earrings that so offended him on their first meeting. She flushes at the memory, and at that point Tesla appears.

"Shall we walk?" he asks.

She nods and matches his stride, careful not to take his arm. Tesla is not comfortable with personal contact.

To their left is the Hall of Agriculture. She has heard that its most popular attraction is an 11-ton cheese from Ontario. Like so many other visitors to the Fair, she has not actually visited any of the exhibits. They seem dull and pedestrian compared to the purity and classical lines of the buildings which house them. The fragrance of fresh roses drifts out through the open doors, and for a moment she is lost in a reverie of New York in the spring.

As they pass the end of the hall they are in darkness for a few moments. Tesla seems to shudder. He has been silent and intent, as if compulsively counting his steps. It would not surprise her if this were actually the case.

"Is anything wrong?" she asks. "No," Tesla says. "It's nothing."

In fact, the darkness is full of lurking nightmares for Tesla. Just now he was five years old again, watching his older brother Daniel fall to his death. Years of guilty self-examination have not made the scene clearer. They stood together at the top of the cellar stairs, and then Daniel fell into the darkness. Did he fall? Did Nikola, in a moment of childish rage, push him?

All his life he has feared the dark. His father took his candles away, so little Nikola made his own. Now the full-grown Tesla has brought electric light to the White City, carried by safe, inexpensive alternating current. It is only the beginning.

They round the East end of the Court of Honor. At the Music Hall, the Imperial Band of Austria plays melodies from Wagner. Anne Morgan shivers in the evening chill. "Look at the moon," she says. "Isn't it romantic?"

Tesla's smile seems condescending. "I have never understood the romantic impulse. We humans are meat machines, and nothing more."

"That is hardly a pleasant image."

"I do not mean to be offensive, only accurate. That is the aim of science, after all."

"Yes, of course," Anne Morgan says. "Science." There seems no way to reach him, no chink in his cool exterior. This is where the others gave up, she thinks. I will prove stronger than all of them. In her short, privileged existence, she has always obtained what she wants. "I wish I knew more about it."

"Science is a pure, white light," Tesla says. "It shines evenly on all things, and reveals their particular truths. It banishes uncertainty, and opinion, and contradiction. Through it we master the world."

They have circled back to the west, and to their right is the Liberal Arts Building. She has heard that it contains so much painting and sculpture that one can only wander helplessly among it. To attempt to seek out a single artist, or to look for the French Impressionists, of whom she has been hearing so much, would be sheer futility.

Under Tesla's electric lights, the polished facade of the building sparkles. For a moment, looking down the impossibly long line of perfect Corinthian columns, she feels what Tesla feels: the triumph of man over nature, the will to conquer and shape and control.

Then the night breeze brings her the scent of roses from across the Basin and the feeling passes.

#

They enter the Electricity Building together and stand in the center, underneath the great dome. This is the site of the Westinghouse exhibit, a huge curtained archway resting upon a metal platform. Beyond the arch are two huge Tesla coils, the largest ever built. At the peak of the arch is a tablet inscribed with the words: WESTINGHOUSE ELECTRIC & MANUFACTURING CO. / TESLA POLYPHASE SYSTEM.

Tesla's mood is triumphant. Edison, his chief rival, has been proven wrong. Alternating current will be the choice of the future. The Westinghouse company has this week been awarded the contract to build the first two generators at Niagara Falls. Tesla cannot forgive Edison's hiring of Menlo Park street urchins to kidnap pets, which he then electrocuted with alternating current—"Westinghoused" them, as he called it. But Edison's petty, lunatic attempts to discredit the polyphase system have failed, and he stands revealed as an old, bitter, and unimaginative man.

Edison has lost, and history will soon forget him.

George Westinghouse himself, Tesla's patron, is here tonight. So are J. P. Morgan, Anne's father, and William K. Vanderbilt and Mayor Harrison. Here also are Tesla's friends Robert and Katharine Johnson, and Samuel Clemens, who insists everyone call him by his pen name.

It is nearly midnight.

Tesla steps lightly onto the platform. He snaps his fingers and gas-filled tubes burst into pure white light. Tesla has fashioned them to spell out the names of several of the celebrities present, as well as the names of his favorite Serbian poets. He holds up his hands to the awed and expectant crowd. "Gentlemen and Ladies. I have no wish to bore you with speeches. I have asked you here to witness a demonstration of the power of electricity."

He continues to talk, his voice rising to a high pitch in his excitement. He produces several wireless lamps and places them around the stage. He points out that their illumination is undiminished, despite their distance from the broadcast power source. "Note how the gas at low pressure exhibits extremely high conductivity. This gas is little different from that in the upper reaches of our atmosphere."

He concludes with a few fireballs and pinwheels of light. As the applause gradually subsides he holds up his hands once again. "These are little more than parlor tricks. Tonight I wish to say thank you, in a dramatic and visible way, to all of you who have supported me through your patronage, through your kindness, through your friendship. This is my gift to you, and to all of mankind."

He opens a panel in the front of the arch. A massive knife switch is revealed. Tesla makes a short bow and then throws the switch.

#

The air crackles with ozone. Electricity roars through Tesla's body. His hair stands on end and flames dance at the tips of his fingers. Electricity is his God, his best friend, his only lover. It is clean, pure, absolute. It arcs through him and invisibly into the sky. Tesla alone can see it. To him it is blinding white, the color he sees when inspiration, fear, or elation strikes him.

The coils draw colossal amounts of power. All across the great hall, all over the White City, lights flicker and dim. Anne Morgan cries out in shock and fear.

Through the vaulted windows overhead the sky itself begins to glow. Something sparks and hisses and the machine winds down. The air reeks of melted copper and glass and rubber. It makes no difference. The miracle is complete.

Tesla steps down from the platform. His friends edge away from him, involuntarily. Tesla smiles like a wise father. "If you will follow me, I will show you what man has wrought."

Already there are screams from outside. Tesla walks quickly to the doors and throws them open.

Anne Morgan is one of the first to follow him out. She cannot help but fear him, despite her attraction, despite all her best intentions. All around her she sees fairgoers with their necks craned upward, or their eyes hidden in fear. She turns her own gaze to the heavens and lets out a short, startled cry.

The sky is on fire. Or rather, it burns the way the filaments burn in one of Tesla's electric lamps. It has become a sheet of glowing white. After a few seconds the glare hurts her eyes and she must look away.

It is midnight, and the Court of Honor is lit as if by the noonday sun. She is close enough to hear Tesla speak a single, whispered word: "Magnificent."

Westinghouse comes forward nervously. "This is quite spectacular," he says, "but hadn't you best, er, turn it off?"

Tesla shakes his head. Pride shines from his face. "You do not seem to understand. The atmosphere itself, some 35,000 feet up, has become an electrical conductor. I call it my 'terrestrial night light.' The charge is permanent. I have banished night from the world for all time."

"For all time?" Westinghouse stammers.

Anne Morgan slumps against a column, feels the cold marble against her back. Night, banished? The stars, gone forever? "You're mad," she says to Tesla. "What have you done?"

Tesla turns away. The reaction is not what he expected. Where is their gratitude? He has turned their entire world into a White City, a city in which crime and fear and nightmares are no longer possible. Yet men point at him, shouting curses, and women weep openly.

He pushes past them, toward the train station. Meat machines, he thinks. They are so used to their inefficient cycles of night and day. But they will learn.

He boards a train for New York and secures a private compartment. As he drives on into the white night, his window remains brilliantly lighted.

In the light there is truth. In the light there is peace. In the light he will be able, at last, to sleep.

##

5

Craft Problems and Solutions

Okay, now that you've read "White City," let's continue …

Educated readers might be expected to know that Thomas Edison didn't invent the electric light, but was credited with making it practical and affordable. These imagined readers *might* also know of his contentious battle with George Westinghouse over the future of electrical distribution, that is, whether Westinghouse's alternating current or Edison's direct current would be the chosen future technology (Urth, par 3). However, it is less likely that they would know of Nikola Tesla, the protagonist of Shiner's story. And it would be even less likely that they would know that the Serbian born genius and prolific inventor had worked for Edison, that during that period of association Tesla discovered and experimented with alternating current, and that it was because of Tesla's patented inventions that Westinghouse won what came to be known as "the War of Currents" (Sandford, par 6).

So for our purposes, we shall assume an educated reader who has never heard of Tesla, but knows that Edison was a real person who had something to do with the light bulb.

First, let us get our bearings by placing Shiner's story in a counterfactual context as per the model assembled in the last chapter: Although the story can be considered a "true counterfactual story" as manifold clues to earlier divergence points are provided in the text, *I* would consider "White City" a nexus story because the major catalyzing divergence point occurs at the moment of the break, that being the moment when Nikola Tesla throws a switch at the Chicago World's Fair and seemingly sets the night sky on fire: "Or rather, it burns the way the filaments burn in one of Tesla's electric lamps. It has become a sheet of glowing white" (Dann, *Guide* 33[1]). Although one might look at this story as eschatological, it being concerned with final events or an ultimate destiny, it really is the opposite: its emphasis, which tips the balance, if you like, is focused on origin, development, and cause, as per Hellekson's model (2). And like Keith Robert's novel *Pavane* discussed earlier, Shiner doesn't use an explanatory trope/device such as a time machine or other such "marvel" to lever the reader into the story, but presents its altering/altered history as a given. The reader is dropped into "the present of the past." She is witness to the moment when Tesla throws the switch into counterfactuality, the moment when history diverges dramatically ... and is also witness to its immediate effect, when Tesla's business partner George Westinghouse nervously approaches him:

> "This is quite spectacular," he says, "but hadn't you best, er, turn it off?"
> Tesla shakes his head. Pride shines from his face. "You do not seem to understand. The atmosphere itself, some 35,000 feet up, has become an electrical conductor. I call it my 'terrestrial night light.' The charge is permanent. I have banished night from the world for all time."
> "For all time?" Westinghouse stammers (Dann, *Guide* 45).

We can thus classify "White City" as a second stage genre construct, á la Russ: plausibility is key, and it is a "What if?" story treated realistically, plausibly, and with complexity.

And, lastly, this story also fits Edgar L. Chapman's postmodern third stage era in its fictional techniques and exploration of problematical political, cultural, and moral issues. As Shiner has written:

> I had been reading for years about Nikola Tesla and, in parallel, about the Columbian Exhibition in Chicago in 1893 ... When my sense of a possible story reached a certain critical mass, I started reading Margaret Cheney's *Tesla: Man Out of Time* (1998). Cheney at one point starts listing all the ideas Tesla had recorded in his notebooks that he never got around

---

[1]All page citations for "White City" refer to its inclusion in this book.

to completing, and one of them was the "Terrestrial Night Light" ... My brain responded like a pinball machine when you've hit the jackpot, with all kinds of buzzers and lights. This was the best example I'd ever heard of science trampling over sentiment simply because it could. It also dovetailed with many of Tesla's personal quirks, and made me understand that, unlike the weirdo hero many people thought Tesla to be, he was, for me, a monster.

The "White City" of the Columbian Exposition seemed to be a similar sort of thing: Art and culture and food and technology from around the world being plundered in the name of modernity and science. What better place for Tesla to carry out his fiendish plan?

In a sense, the resulting story ... is alternate history—obviously Tesla did not create this experiment in our world. *I was not concerned, however, with the point at which our histories diverged—I didn't care why Tesla never completed the experiment, or what would have had to change in history to get him to that point. For me the story functions more as reductio ad absurdum—this is where science, without compassion, leads* (italics mine).

(Dann, *Guide* 110)

Although we might now know what kind of story we are dealing with—and we have the author's explanation of why he wrote it—let us examine exactly how Shiner gives the "educated" reader the information she needs to experience the novum of the divergence point.

But what information *does* the reader need to know?

Just as the writer must always keep in mind the position of the protagonist in relation to other characters and objects; just as she must ask herself what the protagonist sees, hears, smells, and feels at any given moment, so must the story answer who, where, when, what, how, and why.

Who: The first two sentences of the story highlight Tesla's compulsive fastidiousness by focusing on the measurements of a piece of steak he is lifting to his mouth and the subsequent scrubbing of a water spot he notices on his fork. Notice that Tesla picks up a "fresh napkin from the stack at his elbow" (Dann, *Guide* 29). Through this ostensibly throw-away detail, Shiner allows the reader to discover that unlike an ordinary restaurant customer Tesla has demanded a stack of fresh napkins. Rather than telling us who Tesla is, Shiner is *showing* us; and if a writer knows her craft, she should be able to communicate necessary information "under the wire," as it were.

Part of the "toolbox" of science fiction writers, or as Edward James calls it, "the SF writer's art," is knowing how "to introduce the reader to the background by means of clues inserted in the text" (115). Robert Heinlein was the master of this technique, as witnessed by the often quoted line from his novel *Beyond This Horizon* (1948): "the door dilated" (5). In the 1940s that was revelatory, and the technique was subsequently called "Heinleining."

As Harlan Ellison was quoted as saying:

> And no discussion. Just "the door dilated." I read across it, and was two lines down before I realized what the image had been, what the words had called forth. A *dilating* door. It didn't open, it *irized*! Dear God, now I knew I was in a future world.
>
> (qtd. in James 115)

I agree with James when he says that "the decoding and assessment of these clues can be a major part of the pleasure provided by the work; indeed, without that decoding and assessment, in a process of careful reading, it may be impossible to understand the text at all" (115). And you should also note how Shiner utilizes passing references, dialogue, and overt narration to impart necessary information and what we might refer to as personal shading: it is the accretion of details, this mixture of what might be familiar and unfamiliar, which allows the reader to grasp, no matter how imperfectly, the historical context and the novum of the divergence.

In marked contrast to judicious "showing and telling"—to providing information in the form of clues, careful accretion of detail throughout the story, and "biteable" exposition and dialogue—is the information dump: that infelicitous, awkward, and dreaded expository lump.

Vonda McIntyre provided a good, over-the-top example in her excellent blog *Pitfalls of Writing Science Fiction & Fantasy*: "As you know, George, the space station's orbit is degrading rapidly, and we're running out of air" (sec 1). She goes on to write: "Detection trick: If the phrase 'As you know,' or 'As you should know' would make sense in a line of dialogue, the dialogue is probably an expository lump" (sec 1).

To continue: three paragraphs after Tesla has picked up his fresh napkin, Shiner gives us an "external shot" of Tesla from the perspective of J. Pierpoint Morgan's daughter—and the name recognition of the financier should further orient the educated reader. Although Anne Morgan knows he prefers to dine alone, she intrudes upon his privacy because "she is drawn to him irresistibly. He is rake thin and handsome as the devil himself, with steel gray eyes that pierce through to her soul" (Dann, *Guide* 30); and later as they walk together, we are privy to her musings about him:

> At least part of the attraction is the mystery of his personal life. At age thirty-seven he has never married nor been engaged. She has heard rumors that his tastes might be, to put it delicately, Greek in nature. There is no evidence to support this gossip and she does not credit it. Rather it seems likely that no one has yet been willing to indulge the inventor's many idiosyncrasies.
>
> (30)

So having only read the first page of "White City," we know Tesla's age, eccentricities, character, and profession (inventor), as well as the narrative hook that at midnight he will produce his greatest miracle. The reader does not have to know the historical Tesla (yet), although if she does, there will be an added frisson as Tesla was a germaphobe and was reputed to run through seventeen towels a day (Sanford, par 4).

When Tesla and Anne walk into the dark area of a passageway, we learn that Tesla is afraid of the dark because he watched his brother fall to his death down a flight of cellar stairs ... or because he might have pushed him (Dann, *Guide* 31). We learn that he is condescending to Anne and is wedded to science, a cold, isolate idea of science as opposed to any notion of romance because "Science is a pure, white light ... It shines evenly on all things, and reveals their particular truths. It banishes uncertainty, and opinion, and contradiction. Through it we master the world" (31). A cold, isolated, fussy, driven character, Tesla, a man who sees "We humans as meat machines, and nothing more" (31); and by page three we learn that the stadium in which Tesla and Anne are now standing is lit by "*Tesla's* electric lights" (italics mine), and in the Electricity Building, "the site of the Westinghouse exhibit," we see huge Tesla coils and an inscribed plinth: "WESTINGHOUSE ELECTRIC & MANUFACTURING CO./TESLA POLYPHASE SYSTEM" (32).

Why: The why, Tesla's motivation, gives the reader more hooks into the consensual history we are about to leave. As mentioned earlier, he is afraid of the dark: "All his life he has feared the dark. His father took his candles away, so little Nikola made his own. Now the full-grown Tesla has brought electric light to the White City, carried by safe, inexpensive alternating current. It is only the beginning" (31). But Shiner carries this further into a sort of historical nitty-gritty that—along with other specifics to be described—gives the reader enough information, both familiar and perhaps unfamiliar, to grasp the major oncoming divergence point:

> Tesla's mood is triumphant. Edison, his chief rival, has been proven wrong. Alternating current will be the choice of the future. The Westinghouse company has this week been awarded the contract to build the first two generators at Niagara Falls. Tesla cannot forgive Edison's hiring of Menlo Park street urchins to kidnap pets, which he then electrocuted with alternating current—"Westinghoused" them, as he called it. But Edison's petty, lunatic attempts to discredit the polyphase system have failed, and he stands revealed as an old, bitter, and unimaginative man.
>
> Edison has lost, and history will soon forget him.
>
> (Dann, *Guide* 32)

Thus we are *told* that Tesla and Westinghouse and alternating current have won. The tiny frisson, the small novum, is, of course, that history certainly didn't forget Edison. But the *raison d'être* for Tesla creating the major divergence point revealed in this story, his fear of the dark and compulsive need to cleanse himself (light being the ultimate disinfectant), is brought home in the final lines:

> He boards a train for New York and secures a private compartment. As he drives on into the white night, his window remains brilliantly lighted.
>
> In the light there is truth. In the light there is peace. In the light he will be able, at last, to sleep (34).

When and *Where*: Shiner sets the time and place in the second paragraph, economically *showing* the reader the when and where of what was:

> He is sitting at a private table in the refreshment stand at the west end of the Court of Honor. He looks out onto the Chicago World's Fair and Columbian Exposition. It is October of 1893. The sun is long gone and the reflections of Tesla's electric lights sparkle on the surface of the Main Basin, turning the spray from the fountain into glittering jewels. At the far end of the Basin stands the olive-wreathed Statue of the Republic in flowing robes. On all sides the White City lies in pristine elegance, testimony to the glorious architecture of ancient Greece and Rome. Its chilly streets are populated by mustached men in topcoats and sturdy women in woolen shawls.
>
> (29)

And in the next paragraph, as mentioned earlier, we are told what "will be" in the form of a narrative hook: "The time is 9:45. At midnight Nikola Tesla will produce his greatest miracle" (29). Throughout the story, the reader is fed details ("To their left is the Hall of Agriculture. She has heard that its most popular attraction is an 11–ton cheese from Ontario" [30]) and explicit descriptions (see previous), which instruct and situate her in this place and time in what can be understood to be our own consensual history.

How and *What* at this point are obvious even if you have not yet perused the actual story. The major line of demarcation—the Jonbar hinge, the catalyzing divergence point—is brought into existence when Tesla plays God and obliterates night. Once he pulls the switch, the reader cannot help but accept that we are truly in alternity. Tesla tells us how this is accomplished by demonstrating how the light from wireless lamps remains constant when moved away from their source of power and then points out "how the gas at low pressure exhibits extremely high conductivity. This gas is little different from that in the upper reaches of our atmosphere" (32). He literally turns the atmosphere into an electrical conductor: his "terrestrial night light." But the reader doesn't have to know that the "real" Tesla actually conceived of this as a "practical" invention to appreciate the story as counterfactual. [As an aside, the biographer Margaret Cheney called the "terrestrial night light" one of Tesla's "most grandiose inventions" (91). "He saw it as a means of making shipping lanes and airports safer at night, or as a way of illuminating whole cities without the use of street lights ... When asked how he proposed to conduct his currents to the upper air, he merely replied that it did not present any practical difficulties" (92)].

As I hope is now obvious, all the information that the reader needs in order to experience the counterfactual novum is *in* the story. The author has done our homework for us: there is no necessity for external research, other than out of interest as a post-reading activity to gain a greater appreciation of the subject matter.

But what about those stories that depict histories which are not familiar ... and those stories in which the divergence/Jonbar points are not readily apparent: those stories I earlier referred to as being on the far end of the bell-shaped curve?

Before we begin, I would emphasize that the techniques and elements previously described when we deconstructed Lewis Shiner's "White City" are the core tools for informing the reader of the historical background and will work to varying degrees, depending on the skill and inventiveness of the author, whether the historical period of the story is familiar or unfamiliar. The following strategies are simply additional approaches to presenting information; and in most cases their efficacy will be dependent upon the kind and length of the story being told. For example, these techniques (for the most part) are more applicable to novels than to shorter works and include forewords, afterwords, chapter quotes, character and place listings, maps, inserting fictional documents from the period such as letters, newspapers, and advertisements. These devices can act as signposts to help the reader recognize the historical counterfactual branchings and appreciate their attendant novums.

It should also be noted that some of these devices or strategies for acquainting the reader with more outré historical scenarios are less organic than others—and, hence, less useful. Forewords and afterwords, for instance, allow the author to engage with the reader and provide historical context under the pretext, if you will, of personalizing the material by discussing the author's relationship to it. But both are add-ons, rather than organic (intrinsic) components of the novel.

A foreword (or introduction) can certainly draw the reader into the material, but it can just as easily get in the reader's way; and the more likely option is that the reader will skip it entirely. An afterword is "safer" in this respect, but it is by definition *ex post facto*: meant to be read after completion of the novel. However, if the author has done her job and captured the reader's interest, the afterword can certainly add another dimension to the reader's experience. But for *our* purposes that is, in effect, gilding the lily. As expressed earlier didactically and by example (our deconstruction of "White City"), the job of bringing the reader up to speed is best done organically: within the confines and the body of the story itself.

That said, an introduction can give the author a chance, right from the get-go, to "tell" interested readers what they will need to know ... and as an added bonus, introductions and afterwords often act as crib-sheets for overworked reviewers and interviewers!

Another effective device is John Dos Passos' modernist technique of inserting magazine and newspaper clippings, songs, and the like into the text. But this only works if used carefully and judiciously; otherwise, it risks becoming stylistically jarring and intrusive to the modern reader. This device was taken up by New Wave writers such as John Brunner, who famously used it to great effect in his novel *The Sheep Look Up*. Here is a more extreme example from Brunner's book, which, incidentally, is a very fine work, if of its time (1972):

> *Polychlorinated biphenyls: waste products of the plastics lubrication and cosmetics industries. Universal distribution at levels similar to DDT, less toxic but having more marked effect on steroid hormones. Found in museum collected as early as 1944. Known to kill birds.*

Followed by:

> Similarly it's a short mental step from the notion of killing plants or insects to the notion of killing animals and people. It didn't take the Vietnam disaster to spell that out—it was foreshadowed in everybody's mind.

Followed by:

> **FARM & GARDEN INC.**
> Landscaping & Pest Control Experts

You get the idea.

Although they have their limitations, I have also found prefatory character lists to be effective. They provide the reader with a reference to the many characters in a large novel, define unfamiliar terms, and can also act as novums in themselves. A beta-reader queried me on the use of "aeon" in *Shadows in the Stone*: he hadn't heard of the term and thought it might confuse readers, especially as the term was used early in the character list to describe an angelic/demonic being—

> Athoth: A powerful lower aeon who can assume other identities. He is also known as the Whirlwind and the Reaper, and some scriptures represent him (mistakenly) as the dark aeon Belias (1).

—and it also appeared in the novel's introductory quote:

> "Listen to me, Trismegistus. I mean who will he choose to walk beside him in the final struggle against the demiurge and his *aeons*" (italics mine)?

I remedied the problem simply by adding a definition of aeon, which appears as the second alphabetical entry in the character list and, thus, has a better chance of being noticed:

> Aeons: High order angels ... extensions of the highest source of being. Upper aeons are emanations or creations of the true creator known as the Invisible Spirit. Lower aeons are emanations or creations of the demiurge Yaldabaoth (also known as Jehovah), who is himself a lower aeon (1).

Character lists can also provide other clues as to the nature of this counterfactual cosmos. In my novel *The Rebel: Second Chance*, a greatly expanded version of *The Rebel: an Imagined Life of James Dean*, character descriptions provide clues to the counterfactual timeline and possibly create their own small novums:

> *Nixon, Richard*: Presidential hopeful (707)
> *Reagan, Ronald* actor and politician, best known as host of

Death Valley Days and as the villain in *The Killers* (708)

It might be noted that most of my character descriptions hold true in our own timeline, which fosters the sense of verisimilitude and excites pleasure when the reader encounters a counterfactual description. The following is accurate in our timeline:

Strasberg, Lee: the most influential acting teacher of the twentieth century; as artistic director of the Actor's Studio in New York City—of which James Dean, Marilyn Monroe, Marlon Brando, Julie Harris, Montgomery Clift, Al Pacino, Rod Steiger, and Dustin Hoffmann were members—he brought method acting to prominence. As an actor, he is best known for his role as Hyman Roth in *The Godfather Part II* (709)

I have found chapter headings in the form of quotes or extracts from books, reports, newspapers or the like to be very useful ... more useful than the techniques described above for communicating information about a novel's altered history. To my mind chapter headings are less intrusive and invasive than pastiche insertions à la Dos Passos and Brunner because they have the distinct advantage of being part of the text but not *in* the text. The reader, of course, can choose to skim these sections, but I would venture that at least some of the information will "stick."

We might call this the Encyclopedia Galactica device.

The World Heritage Encyclopedia provides a concise history and description of the term "Encyclopedia Galactica":

The concept and name of the *Encyclopædia Galactica* first appeared in Isaac Asimov's short story "Foundation" (*Astounding Science Fiction*, May 1942), later republished as "The Encyclopædists" in the short story collection *Foundation* (1951). Asimov's *Encyclopædia Galactica* was a compendium of all knowledge then available in the Galactic Empire, intended to preserve that knowledge in a remote region of the Galaxy in the event of a foreseen Galactic catastrophe. The Encyclopædia is later revealed to be an element in an act of misdirection, its real purpose being to concentrate a group of knowledgeable scientists on a remote, resource-poor planet, with the long-term aim of revitalizing the technologically stagnant and scientifically dormant Empire. Originally published in a physical medium, it later becomes computerized and subject to continual change.

Asimov used the *Encyclopedia Galactica* as a literary device throughout his *Foundation* series, beginning many of the book sections or chapters with a short extract from the *Encyclopedia* discussing a key character or event in the story.

("Asimov's," par 2)

Here is an example from Asimov's *Foundation* (1951):

COMMISSION OF PUBLIC SAFETY— ... *The aristocratic coterie rose to power after the assassination of Cleon I, last of the Entuns. In the main, they formed an element of order during the centuries of instability and uncertainty in the Imperium. Usually under the control of the great families of the Chens and the Divarts, it degenerated eventually into a blind instrument for maintenance of the status quo ... They were not completely removed as a power in the state until after the accession of the last strong Emperor, Cleon II. The first Chief Commissioner ...*

... In a way, the beginning of the Commission's decline can be traced to the trial of Hari Seldon two years before the beginning of the Foundational Era. That trial is described in Gaal Dornick's biography of Hari Seldon ...
ENCYCLOPEDIA GALACTICA (17–18)

Most practitioners would not want to (blatantly) copy Asimov's style. I adapted it in *Shadows* as a means to convey information by employing quotations from sources such as *The Gnostic Gospels, Dr. John Dee's Action with Spirits, John Dee's Five Books of Mystery,* Thomas Browne's *Religio Medici,* Giordiano Bruno's *Gli Eroici Furori,* and Agrippa of Nettescheim's *Three Books of Occult Philosophy.* In certain instances, I made changes in the quotes to fit the needs of my altered world. So, for example, the line "The root of their tree is bitter, its branches are death ... " from "The Secret Book of John" becomes "The root of the tree of Belias is bitter, its branches are death ... " And in other instances I made up quotes and entire gospels, notably *The Gospel of the Damned* and *The Discourses of Trismegistus and Rheginus*, which function as my own iteration of the *Encyclopedia Galactica* to "explain" *Shadow*'s cosmic history and cosmogony.

To give you an idea of how I have used quotes and "dialogues" to convey information, here is an example from *Shadows*, which fronts the section entitled "Partition One: Soul Stealers":

"Trismegistus, who is the favorite of the demiurge known as Jehovah?"

"It has always been Belias, the aeon of ice and darkness."

"But Trismegistus, is he not also called the betrayer, the adversary? Is he not also known as Satan?"

"Rheginus, Do you question your Catechism?"

"I swear to you, I do not. But many confuse Belias with the one they call Satan."

"Rheginus, listen to me. Of course, the ignorant confuse Belias with the one they call Satan."

"Why, Trismegistus?"

"Because Belias is the one whom the demiurge dispatches to obstruct human activities and desires."
—*Excerpt from the First Discourse47,27–53.14*

"Tell me, Trismegistus. Is the one called Satan an angel or aeon in his own right?"

"I should not laugh at what you say, Rheginus. Yes, Satan is an aeon in his own right."

"Is he, then, the demiurge's adversary?"

"Would you consider your conquered enemy an adversary, Rheginus?"

"No, Trismegistus, not after I had taken his sword and shield."

"And would you not then cast him down and castrate him so that he and his kind could not threaten you again?"

"Yes, of course, Trismegistus."

"Just so, Rheginus, did the demiurge cast down Satan and give him to his favorite aeon Belias to be entombed in his dark, frozen wastes. So now there is only one adversary."

"Who would that be?"

"The adversary of the Invisible One. The adversary of the True God."

"Now I understand, Trismegistus. The adversary of the True God is the demiurge Jehovah."
        —*Excerpt from the First Discourse48,12–53.14*
                (*Shadows* 29–30)

Only you can determine whether this kind of technique/device fits your vision of any given work.

Many techniques and strategies applicable to general fiction can also have specific (if altered) applications to counterfactual fiction, strategies such as the developing of involvement: I'm directing myself here to development, reiteration, and extension of history and background. As Albert Van Nostrand wrote in *The Denatured Novel*, a critical study which had top-of-mind awareness at the time (1960) and which I still think resonates today:

> This developing of involvement is a way of making the most of the least material. In painting, for example, a basic fact of composition is that the parts repeat one another, not literally but with variations. In music, sequential treatment repeats a motif elsewhere on the scale, or by another voice or instrument. The most familiar form of repetition in orchestral scores is the theme-and-variations, although its most intense use is probably in the fugue, which counterpoints its parts. And so in fiction: the novel builds a system of comparisons; its conflicts test opposing values and also, by analogy, one another. Like parallelism in painting or sequential treatment in music, the dynamics of a novel exceeds mere restatement for its own sake, but uses it variously to develop an idea. And appraisal inheres in development.
>
>   (36)

He also wrote that fiction "is a bizarre exaggeration of mere actuality" (34). This is interesting when one applies it to counterfactual fiction:

> The author must exaggerate in order to communicate at all; otherwise his fiction would not be necessary or believable. But it still must satisfy one's knowledge of the way things happen or one's feeling that they could not have been otherwise, given what one knows or learns about the characters. Therefore, a kind of necessity or inevitability rules it, in that the action follows given conditions, and nothing else could have happened.
>
> (34)

However, before we leave this topic, I'd like to turn everything I've previously said about "telling" on its head—I'm referring here to expository lumps, specifically narrative lumps.

When you begin to write a book, you are also automatically making decisions pertaining to your audience. How financially rewarding a counterfactual project might be can depend on the difficulty of the material, the demands it makes upon the reader. And as noted earlier, writing about a well-known personage or period of history will certainly expand the audience; and material that can also involve young adults has the potential to enlarge the audience again.

Or as Madeleine L'Engle wrote, "You have to write the book that needs to be written. And if the book will be too difficult for grownups, then you write it for children" ("9 Thoughts", par 2).

However, if you as a writer are caught by an idea, an idea that demands the kind of complexity that puts more than ordinary demands on the reader, an idea that is historically esoteric, such as Ekaterina Sedia's *Heart of Iron* or Kingsley Amis's masterpiece of counterfactual fiction *The Alteration* (1976), that work *may* not find a mass audience. But—and it's a big but—the audience for your book may be more willing to accept difficulty ... may be willing to accept more density of prose, more structural complexity, and, yes, even what we might consider narrative lumps. I'm referencing this as a matter of style. Such density certainly doesn't fit most accessible prose styles, nor should it(!); but it does fit some, and I'm referring here to Kingsley Amis's brilliant novel *The Alteration*.

Like Keith Roberts's *Pavane*, *The Alteration* takes place in a counterfactual branching where the Catholic Church is all-powerful. In *Pavane*'s continuum Queen Elizabeth was assassinated in 1588; in the continuum of *The Alteration* the Reformation failed and Martin Luther became Pope. Although Amis's novel opens into a world that feels medieval, the reader encounters a series of small, brilliant novums such as mosaics by Hockney and frescos by Blake in St. George's cathedral before she is told that "In the year of Our Lord one thousand nine hundred and seventy-six, Christendom would see nothing more mournful or more stately" (12).

I will leave you to make up your own mind as to whether the following "lump" inserted into an after-hours intertextual discussion of "Counterfeit World" fiction that takes place among preteen boys in a monastery stops or enhances the reading experience—and if, indeed, it is a lump:

> "Flying-machines always appear—this is no more than ordinary TR," growled Decuman. "You said it was CW."
>
> TR, or Time Romance, was a type of fiction that appealed to a type of mind. It had readers among schoolboys, collegiates, mechanics, inventors, scribes, merchantmen, members of Convocation and even, it was whispered, those in holy orders. Though it was formally illegal, the authorities were wise enough to know that to suppress it altogether a disproportionate effort would be necessary, and contented themselves with occasional raids and confiscations. Its name was the subject of unending debate among its followers, many of whom would point to the number of stories and novels offered and accepted as TR in which time as such played no significant part. The most commonly suggested alternative, Invention Fiction, made a beguiling acronym, but was in turn vulnerable to the charge that invention was no necessary ingredient of TR. (Science was a word and idea considered only in private: who would publish a bawdy pamphlet under the heading of *Disgusting Stories?*) CW or Counterfeit World, a class of tale set more or less at the present date, but portraying the results of some momentous change in historical fact, was classified as TR by plenty of others besides Decuman, if on no firmer grounds than the writers of one sometimes ventured into the other.

Thomas answered Decuman's objection. "Wait: what has happened is first of all that the Holy Victory never took place" (27).

To my mind this is, indeed, a narrative lump ... but what a glorious one! And I would also note that this is a problem with laying down rules: the exceptions often prove to be far more interesting than the accepted standards.

#

Okay, let's get our bearings ...

We've looked at some of the problems involved in the craft of writing counterfactual fiction, concentrating on the contentious issue of reader unfamiliarity with the counterfactual departures from consensual history. And I've outlined how you might acquaint a naive reader with the details and history surrounding a chosen divergence point without forcing the reader to go outside of the text of the story. Then we deconstructed Lewis Shiner's counterfactual short story and began to transform abstract theory into practical, specific craft solutions and strategies. Those craft solutions and strategies form part of what I'm calling the counterfactual toolbox. These solutions include:

1   Choosing a divergent point that the average reader can recognize.

2   An acute mindfulness on the part of the writer regarding the historical knowledge of the reader.

3   Employing paratextual elements, including forewords, afterwords, chapter quotes, character and place listings, maps, and the insertion of fictional documents including letters, newspapers, and advertisements.

4   Describing familiar places and characters which may have different characteristics and functions in the counterfactual story world.

5   Implementing the technique of Heinleining, which involves providing concise but necessary details in the form of clues without distorting the narrative. Indeed, it is hoped that decoding the clues becomes part of the pleasure provided by the work.

6   Bringing a story to life by selecting and emphasizing certain specific details of an imagined world to create an illusion of coherence and complexity that is experienced as "real," rather than "dumping" information. Although the inclusion of specific detail can be enjoyed with or without an understanding of the historical context, it should be noted that this technique of employing a knowledgeable layering of well-chosen details can become a powerful tool to structure a reader's understanding of even outré consensual history and to aid in the suspension of disbelief.

Allow me to elaborate a bit on this point by mentioning Patrick O'Brian's Aubrey/Maturin series of historical novels. I often use his work when I'm conducting SF writing workshops because, to my mind, they exemplify the techniques of employing specific, focused details to create authentic story worlds. His novels "feel" absolutely authentic because of his obviously rigorous research and what Irving Howe calls a "thickness of specification" (185) which O'Brian achieves through an accretion of detail.

His story worlds are in fact so detailed that they function as characters to create an overarching narrative drive that fuels all of the novels in the series. O'Brian uses a technique akin to Heinlein's of inserting clues into the text; but the "clues" are often a profusion of often undefined nautical terms, which the reader simply accepts and comprehends by association.

To quote A. S. Byatt, the Booker Award-winning author of *Possession: a Romance*: "An essential of the truly gripping book for the narrative addict is the creation of a whole, solidly living world for the imagination to inhabit, and O'Brian does this with prodigal *specificity* [italics mine] and generosity" (*Complete Aubry/Maturin*: 3, inside flap jacket).

#

Next ...

The following chapter will elaborate on craft solutions and strategies and introduce four of my own "rules" that form the basis of an extended Q & A interview with some of the major authors of counterfactual fiction.

This Q & A is basically a seminar on alternate history: what it is and how to do it. Oh, I might also mention that disagreement will be a yeasty and vital ingredient in this discussion.

So now let's hear from some other people.

##

6

The Tactics of Creating Counterfactual Texts

A Roundtable Q & A

This Q & A was conducted several years ago, and this is its first publication. Sadly, one of my contributors, Mary Rosenblum, has passed away. You might have noticed that this book is dedicated to her memory. You might also notice that I have quoted several of the authors' responses in previous chapters to emphasize or reinforce various ideas concerning the craft and character of counterfactual fiction. I would just consider these repetitions as providential *aide-mémoires*.

As you peruse the authors' reactions and responses, you'll get— or you should get—a visceral sense of the diversity of opinion on what constitutes counterfactual fiction and how the craft might and should be approached. This chapter constitutes, in fact, a practical, warts-and-all seminar on the theory and craft of writing counterfactual fiction.

Lastly, the set of concepts described below should be considered as broad conceptual additions to the solutions and strategies enumerated in the last chapter.

\#

As a jumping-off point, I've formulated a set of concepts that *I* think are central to the craft. I'm calling these ideas "concepts" rather than "rules" because they are more general and embracing than, for example, a rule that a divergence point in a counterfactual fiction "should be (1) plausible, (2) definite, (3) small in itself, and (4) massive in consequence" (Shippey 17).

a) *Counterfactual fiction is defined by its relation to history and comes into being through the practitioner's choice of a divergence point.* Divergence points (or Jonbar hinges) may be observed or assumed, and their consequences may range from a present shaped by the allies losing the Second World War or the South winning the American Civil War to entirely altered worlds and ontologies.

b) *The author's research into historical texts not only drives narrative, but creates narrative.* Initial and ongoing research creates new plot branchings, surprising character interactions, and can often strengthen and focus (lagging) narrative momentum.

c) *The story world that emerges from the author's historical research and subsequent creation and extrapolation of narrative can function as a character itself to drive action.* In mimetic contemporary fiction, the story world—the place and time—are generally familiar and do not require basic explanation to be understood and imagined by the reader. However, in counterfactual fiction, just as in most speculative and historical fiction, the story world is to varying degrees estranged from our known world; and this implied and explicit estrangement takes up a similar affective and tropological "space" to other characters in a given work.

d) *These invented story worlds are brought to life by a technique that I'll refer to as "layering."* Layering is the technique of selecting and emphasizing certain specific details of an imagined world to create an illusion of coherence and complexity that is experienced as "real"— what Irving Howe refers to as "thickness" of specification (185)—thus facilitating the reader's willing "suspension of disbelief."

Would you consider any (or all) of these "concepts" as being central to creating alternate history?

Andrew Enstice: First, I should probably say that writing counterfactual history must always—as Shippey implies—involve a high degree of self-awareness in the writing process. But trying to couch my responses in terms of Shippey's definitions has proved quite challenging.

Yes, in developing our counterfactual history *The Five Star Republic*, Janeen Webb and I began with a notional divergence point—in our case, the 1872 completion of the telegraph link between London and Melbourne, Australia. Janeen and I have worked together a great deal over the years, mostly researching and writing literary social history. In the course of this work we came across the very first telegrams sent by that high-tech 1872 link. News that had taken weeks to reach Australia suddenly arrived in less than twelve hours: news of widespread strikes; news of the threat from a brand-new German empire fresh from military victory over France. In Australia, faced with threats that were no longer safely removed in both time and space, local newspapers responded in true Chicken Little style. According to them, the sky above imperial Britain was about to fall.

So our question was: what if that had been true, and not just panic? What if the Empire were falling?

Sounds like a good divergence point. But by the time we'd finished, it turned out to be little more than a footnote to our counterfactual history. There was no specific divergence point at all. Divergence came from multiple sources, dependent not on our mechanical intervention in history, but on subtle shifts in the interactions of historical characters and events produced by throwing historically plausible fictional elements into the mix.

Rather than a divergence point, we had a question: given the state of solar steam technology at the time, and the obvious suitability of the Australian climate for its development, were there any circumstances under which that technology might have become a rival to fossil fuel in the nineteenth century?

Which brings me to Shippey's point B (and, indirectly, C): research.

Yes, yes, and yes! The research necessary to construct a simulacrum of society and events of the time throws up endless nuggets of narrative gold. The counterfactual story comes into existence as a result of that research, filtered through the characters (both historical and fictional). Events unfold as a result of the interaction between these characters and their distinctive fictional world.

John Birmingham: Point A seems to be unavoidable, if you don't have a divergence point, even one that exists only off the page and in the author's private knowledge, then you don't have alternate history. You have fantasy.

Point B. Totally. In fact, it can be a struggle to stop the research from overpowering the story. You can see this happening sometimes in Eric Flint's 1630s series, where it's obvious he has drilled so deep into his period research that the pressure of this blows back up into his face and all over the page. I still love the books, but find myself skipping over whole pages and sections occasionally because I can see it coming. Having said that, the 1630s novels are also an excellent example of how the research becomes the story. Flint's immersion in the source material is so great that the granular details seem to have bonded with the story arc at a molecular level.

I've seen the same thing in my own work more than once, especially in the World War series. That era of modern history has been so thoroughly documented at such insane depth and breadth that it was impossible not to stumble across stories that forced themselves into my narrative. Sometimes this would happen at the macro level, say in the Battle of Midway/the Transition, and sometimes at the micro level when the biographies or autobiographies of individuals might lend themselves to entirely new and emergent storylines. An example of this in *Weapons of Choice* was discovering the autobiography of the writer Peter Ryan which included long descriptions of a trek he undertook to spy on the Japanese in New Guinea. I used Ryan as a character, and tried to infuse my own writing with as much of his point of view and real-world recollections as possible. From that choice, the entire superstructure of the trilogy changed as narrative arcs curved off in different directions from those I had intended.

Point C. I can't speak so much to the work of other alternate history writers, except perhaps Steve Stirling with whom I share a friendship off the page as well as a collegiate relationship on it. But yes, if I get where you're going with this question, the story world itself becomes a character. It might seem like a bit of a reach or even a wank but of course literary critics have been attributing this power to the better crime writers for the decades. Raymond Chandler's Los Angeles, Ian Rankin's Edinburgh, Peter Corris's Sydney, they are all characters in and of themselves. Those cities have history, personality, and motivations independent of the individuals who populate them in those stories. In fact, it is often the case that the cities can be said to have created the characters, for the characters could not exist in exactly the form they do in any other environment. The city, or the world, enables them. The same thing takes place in alternate histories, and I think Stirling's work is probably a much more appropriate example of this than mine. The post-technology feudal world of his *Emberverse* series can be seen changing the psychology and nature of the characters across the decades covered in his books. Indeed, many of the older characters, who grew up in the pre-Event world repeatedly and explicitly comment on the way the changed world is changing the people within it.

Point D. Totes, as the kids say. For me, the layering, the daubing on of little points of detail to build up the reality like a pointillist is half the fun. First in selecting those details from the period being written about, and then applying the force created at the point of divergence to force them into some new and fantastic shape. The further you get from the stories origin point, the more these effects can be seen. One of the reasons I have returned to the alternate world created in *Weapons of Choice* is to see how those forces have changed things a decade after the final book in that series wrapped up.

Michael Bishop: [*As Michael's responses are of a piece and cannot easily be separated into question categories, I have placed his response under the category "Anything else come to mind?"*]

Terry Bisson: (a) Divergence point and also divergence cause. For me it means you are limited to the Real world and Real history. Lincoln fighting zombies is not alternate history, nor are dragons dogfighting Spads. Thus I exclude Fantasy, but also certain SF tropes: Time machines, AK-47s at Gettysburg, etc. Alternate history, not alternate Reality. I am only interested in working with real history.

(b) For me the research is over before the narrative begins. I am somewhat of a purist (minimalist) in that the later changes must all follow from the One Initial Divergence. (Or 3! see below)

(c) The story world is the point of the whole thing. It's more than just a plot-driver.

(d) Ditto the "layering" (which I think of as "art direction.") The details do more than suspend disbelief, they are what the story is about.

John Crowley: They all seem to me both perspicacious as analysis and generative as notions for writers to ponder. It seems to me that a writer of alternate-history fiction has almost a greater responsibility for that "thickness" of specification you speak of than does the creator of—well, what's the name for non-alternate-history fiction? "Standard"? "Common"? "Mimetic"? (No, that last would be entirely wrong, for the AH fiction has to be in a sense MORE mimetic in order to be convincing at all.)

Paul Di Filippo: I find these to be a very cogent and accurate set of principles, Jack! I've encountered instances of all of them in my own alternate-history writing.

William Gibson: I discovered science fiction shortly before I discovered modern history. I read some 1940s SF in the early 1960s before I had any real grasp of, say, the Second World War. I remember reverse-engineering some history from what Heinlein, say, hadn't gotten right about the year I was living in. He had that chart of his imagined future history in each of his paperbacks. I saw that some of it had already become alternate, in the meantime.

We had mandatory state history courses in public school, in Virginia. We used a text approved by the state. History: that slavery hadn't been all that bad at all. So I got it, with some early help from science fiction, that history itself is at best a speculative discipline. That it's malleable.

We don't see the Victorians as they saw themselves, at all, nor as the inhabitants of our own future will see them.

Lisa Goldstein: I've only written one alternate-history story, "Paradise Is a Walled Garden," so I'm not sure how much input I can give here. That said, I definitely had a "Jonbar point" for when history branched, but it turned out to be far too complicated to explain within the framework of the story and I was only able to mention parts of it. Still, it helped me to know what had happened, and to be able to visualize how history would have progressed from there.

Historical research definitely played a large part in the story. I wanted to write about a Spain that had not been reconquered by Christians but had stayed Muslim, and my biggest problem was that I was unable to find good histories that dealt with this. (In fact, you come into this story peripherally—you once asked me for a story with a Jewish theme, and I remembered that I'd read that Jews had fared much better in Muslim Spain than in Christian countries during the Middle Ages. I got several books on the subject but none of them told me what I wanted to know—one of them, in fact, was written by a Jesuit who sounded absolutely delighted at the *Reconquista*. It was only much later that the books I needed started coming out. And that's why I didn't send you a story, actually.)

I didn't use a lot of details from history, though, once I finally found the books I needed. I'd had a sense of what I wanted the world to look like from the beginning, and what I needed mostly was the feel of Muslim Spain, what its daily life looked like. Also, I wanted to make sure my invented world didn't contradict anything from history—or even today, in terms of how a Muslim would practice his/her religion.

As for layering, I hope I was able to do this. I wanted to create a world that would evoke a sense of difference, of the science-fictional "sense of wonder," but to also have enough familiar details to intermittently remind the reader of our own world.

Richard Harland: I'm going to be the fly in the ointment, Jack, because I make use of alternate history tropes in a very different way to you. Of the four concepts above, I strongly agree with (c)—an excellent formulation of the principle! I think I agree with (d), perhaps all the more so because it focuses on a suspension of disbelief through the internal qualities of the created world rather than a power of conviction borrowed from a connection to real-world history. I think (d) works for all fantasy world creation—and my kind of alternate history is definitely a form of fantasy.

I don't feel that concepts (a) and (b) apply to the alternate history I write. As regards (a), well, I didn't start with a divergence point at all when writing *Worldshaker*. I always intended to find a POD to justify my steampunk fantasy world as a form of alternate history, but it wasn't until I approached the key chapters (where Septimus and Professor Twillip uncover the hitherto hidden past) that I started work on a particular justification. My POD wasn't a starting-point, but a means to explain a world that had already grown up on its own.

Similarly, as regards (b). For the juggernaut novels, I had enough general historical knowledge to come up with a recollection that someone had suggested digging a tunnel under the English Channel in Napoleonic times; the only research needed was to fill out the details of the engineer involved and the actual historical moment when he broached his proposal to Napoleon. But did it have to be that particular moment when juggernaut history diverged from real history? I don't think so. Any method of invading England would have served equally well. I just found the idea of hand-digging a tunnel under the Channel intrinsically interesting.

My POD certainly links to the current situation on board the juggernaut, i.e. the Filthies are descended from the working class rebels imprisoned when General Arthur Wellesley overcame the invading army and its local supporters. But it's a very long link—and it doesn't affect anything further in the narrative of *Worldshaker*. The development of the story was already in place before I came up with the POD.

Maybe I'll qualify that later: there were potentials in the alternate long ago past that generated consequences in the sequel, *Liberator*, and even more for *Song of the Slums*, which is set in the same world but only forty-odd years after the POD.

I think the length of time elapsed after the POD is crucial. Nearly two hundred years separate my POD from the juggernaut world of *Worldshaker* and *Liberator*—and almost anything can happen in two hundred years. A lot can happen in 40 years too (think back 40 years from the present—and who would have ever imagined the dissolution of Communism or the rise of neo-medieval Islamic fundamentalism?) Cut to a time lapse of just a few years, and then it's a different story.

Charlaine Harris: I hadn't consciously spelled these out to myself before, but yes, I would. It was relatively easy to pick the divergence point for the *Sookie Stackhouse* novels: vampires have decided to make their existence public. Choosing the place where my history diverged from "real" history required a lot more thought and research for the *Gunnie Rose* books. Though I am not the only writer to choose this event, the most opportune choice for me was the attempted assassination of F. D. Roosevelt in Miami, prior to his taking office as president. Considering all the very serious problems facing the US at or around that point in time, the loss of his leadership would have been crucial. I did have many disasters coincide (more than they actually did in real time) to create the loss of America as an entity.

John Kessel: These concepts seem to me to be relevant to the construction of alternate history fiction. It is true that the more one researches a particular moment in history, learning about individuals, actions, choices made, other circumstances that affected the outcome as we know it, the second concept you posit here comes into play. Real history offers up possibilities that are useful in developing the initial premise of the story.

Some of them, like concept C, seem to me to be the general rule of science fiction writing, where often the setting or background, which may arise from some scientific extrapolation or speculation, becomes an active element in the story. The only difference is that in alternate history, this background comes from the altered events.

Christopher Priest: No.

The opening part of your questionnaire leaves me a bit cold, I'm afraid. I've never accepted the Aldiss/Shippey theory of the single divergent point. Their theory reminds me of those how-to books written by Hollywood screenplay gurus, who do brilliant extraction exercises on what they see as successful scripts, yet haven't the faintest idea how create such a thing and in fact can't tell you. (Offhand, I can't think of a single example of counterfactual fiction written by Aldiss—can you?) History is too complex and has too many large engines running for it to be subverted by a single incident. For instance, you say in your document "a present shaped by the allies losing World War II"— you see, I would contest even that. Although there was a clear military outcome, I'd say that in political, social and economic terms it's still far too soon to see what the real result was, which side "lost," and so on.

Kim Stanley Robinson: Yes, especially a, c, and d. My definition is that alternative histories show us that real history was as we know it, up to a certain point, when things went differently. This point (and I don't like that name "Jonbar point which strikes me as too cutesy and insular to SF fandom) should be identifiable, one way or another, or at least inferable; and what kind of difference it is will tend to define at least part of the writer's theory of history; was it great man stuff? Or a "for loss of a nail the shoe was lost" etc. type theory, maybe out of chaos theory? and so on.

I would definitely agree with the part of c that says that the altered history then becomes a major "character" in the narrative that follows. In other words, if the altered history is just a backdrop for a very conventional tale that doesn't illuminate the changed world (see Len Deighton's *SS GB* for an example) then it is misusing the form.

As for d, yes I agree, and have heard this called "thick texture." I would also add here that I myself make a distinction between "counter-factuals," which is something historians do, as in the books of essays by various historians postulating this change or that, with the essay being a "thin description" that merely summarizes the "what-if" of the change and its consequences; on the other hand, "alternative history" or "alternate history," which comes out of the science fiction tradition, practices "thick texture" and gives the reader the lived experience of the altered history, so the reader can judge it for plausibility, historical effects, or what not. I would add here that counter-factuals are nearly useless, because we have no strong theories of history (not having any controls or comparisons), whereas alternative histories can be rather great, as they immerse us in lifelike considerations of why history happens the way it does.

Mary Rosenblum: I feel that all four of these concepts are critical elements of alternate history in fiction, but the one that I personally feel is the strongest is the emergence of the alternate event-line as "character" in the work. As we reshape history, the new combination of events and individuals changes the tenor of that historical period and, I feel, in the strongest works of historical fiction, creates a viable history that begins to drive the plot and character interactions. Just as the most powerful works of fiction create a perfect balance of plot, the setting, and the characters, that new setting of the alternate history world must balance with plot and character and thus, has a strong influence on both. But this is true with the best SF as well, where the dimensional SF world shapes the plot and characters so that all three aspects of the work balance. Once the historical world is created, for me, certain character behaviors or plot diversions no longer suit the story and it changes.

Pamela Sargent: Yes.

Mark Sherrifs: Yes.

Research certainly creates narrative—or plot as I usually call it.

The story world, or location of the story, can certainly act as a character. I'm reminded of the times I have visited a filming location, prior to or during shooting, and discovered ideas for plot as a result of seeing the unique physical opportunities that the location possesses.

A story world that operates in a particular way can present obstacles and opportunities for story in the same way as a character.

A further thought on this—a character usually requires an intention. It's hard to imagine a story world having an intention, although I just thought of a scenario in which a spaceman crashes on a high gravity planet. The spaceman wants to get off the planet but the high gravity prevents him. Therefore, one might say that the high gravity planet's intention is to keep the spaceman from getting off.

Lewis Shiner: [*As Lewis Shiner's responses (like Michael Bishop's) are of a piece and cannot easily be separated into question categories, I have placed his essay response under the category "Anything else come to mind?"*]

Bruce Sterling: Well, that depends on the resemblance of the narrative at hand to written history. If you're trying to write fake history, then yes, there's a certain elegance in making a small alteration with a large consequence. But I'm not sure that counterfactual fiction needs to mimic history. Historical writing doesn't read much like fiction—history doesn't have page-turning qualities, narrative arcs, catharsis, character transformations, all of that.

Michael Swanwick: For others, perhaps. For myself, foremost is the concept of alternate history as a literary form. So, having come up with a seed idea, the second step would be to think of stories or novels that have dealt with the form in a manner that might make a good rough model. Poul Anderson's "Eutopia," first published in *Dangerous Visions*, would serve as a good example of how to create a varied and Balkanized America, for example. A dystopic alternate history might be written with a heightened awareness of Orwell's *1984* or Walter M. Miller's *A Canticle for Leibowitz*. Both of which, incidentally, are works which were not originally alternate history but with passing time have become such.

I wouldn't actually reread any of these works, however, unless one had solved some very particular plot problem that was giving me trouble, because I have no desire to write something similar to another writer's vision. The exemplar would be the literary equivalent of the wooden mannequin that artists use to set up poses.

Harry Turtledove: Central? I don't think in such terms. Nothing is central to a story except plot, characters, and style, not necessarily in that order at all. I do think it's hard to write a-h—or any other SF or fantasy—as good as mainstream fiction because of the worldbuilding you have to do. As you say, one can't assume things in such tales.

Janeen Webb: A. I agree that counterfactual fiction is defined by its relationship with known historical events. But I disagree about the necessity for a single divergence point. *The Five Star Republic* (co-authored with Andrew Enstice) does not have a single definitive divergence point—rather, it uses a series of small, perfectly possible changes to produce a totally divergent outcome. Known historical events remain the same, but we changed the responses to them (and if the recent pandemic has taught us anything at all, it's that different political, social and scientific responses to exactly the same set of circumstances produce wildly different results).

B. I see this as quintessentially important. History is never fixed, but, over time, certain versions of major events become the received wisdom standardized in secondary texts. That's why I never use them. Original research always throws up alternate versions— often what *almost* happened. Different points of view come to light, revealing how opposing forces interpreted events in the light of what constituted "common knowledge" at the time. Working with official documents, letters and diaries, popular newspaper accounts and so on gives me a feel for what was understood as the reality of the day, and that is often very different from what turns up later as recorded history. It seems obvious, but it's probably worth noting that researching alternate sources generates alternate narratives.

Original research also provides a window into the personal predilections of the people who created the historical events in question: the more we learn about historical personages through reading the documents, diaries and letters they left behind, the easier it is to bring them to life as characters in the counterfactual historical universe. We hear them speak, we see the ink blots of their frustrations, we notice their recurring linguistic idiosyncrasies—it's all grist to the narrative mill in creating believable storylines.

C. I do think that the estranged story world helps to drive the action, particularly as the characters who inhabit it must deal with different sets of complexities. I find that this varies in degree: in *The Five Star Republic*, a radically new City is being built in the Australian desert and dependent upon solar powered steam energy, so everyone involved with it is negotiating an historically divergent set of possibilities; whereas the Melbourne/New York/London-based characters are living in accurately described cities of the time, and have only to navigate the political changes emergent from the development of solar generated electricity.

D. I write like an Impressionist artist, layering up details to create the feel of the story. All those tiny points and all those little details create perspective and build up to a narrative picture. The details are drawn from hugely diverse sources—eyewitness accounts, eulogies, court records, drawings and paintings, music and poetry, menus and cookery books, and so on, as well as from more traditional materials. It is important for me to engage all the reader's senses, so I read widely in the literature of the period to get a feel for the details that were important for contemporary writers at the time.

George Zebrowski: (Regarding [b]:) Yes, real history can be suggestive of plots and character interactions; but more than anything it shows us the immense inertia of human history, its resistance to novel changes. In my novel *Stranger Suns*, my characters shuffle through alternate histories looking for the progressive ones. There are no utopias, they note. They all destroy themselves because in essence all the infinity of variants are one and the same. Utopian variants might exist on an axis away from the main line.

(Regarding [c]:) Yes. The "character" of human variants in *Stranger Suns* reflects Juan Obrion's vast disappointment with his kind.

Would you have "top-of-mind" awareness of any of these concepts when you're engaged in writing or planning an alternate history story or novel?

John Birmingham: I suppose it's like anything you can practice. Initially your awareness is conscious and even forced as you actively apply yourself to world building and firing up the story engine. But eventually that awareness and element of conscious choice will slip into the background as you become more familiar with the story world and it begins to create itself in a process of narrative metastasis. I don't think the awareness of making these choices and using these techniques is ever far from your mind, and there will be many moments during the course of the writing day when you will actively choose to employ them, but the balance will change over the course of the day and a life.

John Crowley: I don't think I have ever actually planned an AH story or novel *as such*: mine are less classifiable. But certainly the duty to create thickness of specification was at the top of my mind in creating my novel about Lord Byron's novel, and in *Four Freedoms*, about an imagined bomber plant in the Second World War—these however were novels in which a new item or device or person is inserted into our common history: a different kind of book. For the history in my *Aegypt* series, my intent was twofold. One was to learn enough about the belief-systems and knowledge-systems of the past that I could make convincing my assertion that once upon a time these ideas and practices and visions did operate in the world. The other was to learn enough of the common life of the times to create that "thickness" even in a world run by magic, angels, and the stars.

Paul Di Filippo: I do believe I am generally a "conscious" writer rather than an "intuitive" one, and so I would indeed be explicitly following these four principles as I write.

William Gibson: Bruce (Sterling) was very good at setting perimeters for our shift off the assumed course of history, so I didn't worry about that. I dove instead into the unofficial, the forgotten, the bad journalism, advertising, diaries of eccentrics ... Looking for the actual techno-shock batshit PTSD quivers of the thing. What history, constantly emergent, tells us increasingly that they were about.

Lisa Goldstein: Definitely kept the Jonbar point in mind. Also as I said above, I tried to keep in mind actual history to make sure I didn't contradict any of it, and, when my imagined history continued on from there, to make sure the feel of it stayed consistent with what had actually happened.

Charlaine Harris: Yes. While the *Sookie* novels were "current history plus supernatural creatures," the *Gunnie Rose* books are much more complicated. I had to anchor Lizbeth's world (North America in the nineteen thirties) by means of learning what households were like then, and tweak them to reflect the changes I was making in society and history.

John Kessel: Certainly the conscious choice of and research on a divergence point is central to my writing in this area.

Christopher Priest: Awareness, yes, but only as a part of everything else.

Kim Stanley Robinson: I wrote three alternative histories, two of them short stories ("The Lucky Strike" and "Vinland the Dream") one of them a long novel (*The Years of Rice and Salt*). With that novel done, I felt I was done with alternative history as a sub-genre (I may have one more someday, but it has to be written as a play, which I can't do until "retirement"). So there are few samples in my work, and it is all in the past for me.

It's also true that I have a story in the form of an essay or meditation, called "A Sensitive Dependence on Initial Conditions," that comments on "the Lucky Strike" and contains all my ideas about history and alternative history, so I direct you to that story for a fuller exposition of most of these ideas of mine.

What I can say now is, I was very aware that my alternative history stories were being written to illustrate the changed historical path I was introducing with the story. I was aware I was proposing also a kind of theory as to how history is made by people. The historical situation was definitely the "major character" in all three works, especially the short stories. However, in "The Lucky Strike" and in *The Years of Rice and Salt*, I wanted to think about the question, what kind of people make historical differences? In "The Lucky Strike" it was a particular kind of character (imaginative, a book reader) placed in an unusually sensitive position by accident. In *Years* there were three character types (activist, conciliator, scientist) who interacted to make things change.

Mary Rosenblum: Besides the power of the created world to shape plot and character interaction, I consciously work at creating a rich, three-dimensional world that will "ring true" to readers. That means incorporating the details of place and society that are documented in such a way that they seem to create a complete tapestry of reality. By focusing attention on valid details of life and place and drawing attention away from details that are less verifiable, the end result is the impression of a detailed and in-depth world even though not all facts needed to actually create a completely three dimensional world exist. That is, in my opinion, a critical aspect of the story. Once readers stumble on a clear anachronism or detail that is clearly not accurate, that fragile and necessary suspension of disbelief shatters and the world's credibility is lost, becoming only a two-dimensional backdrop for an unreal story. Reality depends on that intact suspension that permits readers to believe in the world the author creates.

Pamela Sargent: If you're asking whether or not I was conscious of all of these concepts before beginning to write, or while writing, I'd have to say I was only partly (or unconsciously) aware of them at the time. Looking at your list "after the fact," I seem to have been aware of all of them to some degree. But having to follow any set of rules "consciously" while writing would be stifling, at least for me.

Mark Shirrefs: As a novice writer, possibly. As an experienced story teller, these concepts become instinctive. Rather like playing the music instead of the notes.

Bruce Sterling: I happen to be writing a counterfactual history now, and I've decided not to reveal the Jonbar change. Why does the reader care, exactly? How would the characters in a counterfactual history ever know what was counterfactual about it? From their point of view, it's not "history," it's just events going on within their lives.

Tim Powers used to talk about "card tricks in the dark"— clever things that amuse the author that he doesn't reveal to the reader. I used to think that this was perverse, but lately I've thought differently.

The novel *Difference Engine* by William Gibson and myself has a number of in-jokes that work for a contemporary audience, but that make no sense to the protagonists of the book. Where do these wry remarks come from, within the book's narrative space? There's an inconsistency here that still bothers me. Who is this doubly omniscient narrator who somehow has two histories in his head?

Why does the reader have to share that? The characters don't know it, so why are the characters and readers manipulated on the page in that way?

Michael Swanwick: No more than I would have "top-of-mind" awareness of grammar, basic plotting technique, or means of creating plausible characterization. All these things were mastered and internalized long ago and are used in the service of the work.

Harry Turtledove: I've certainly had it happen that things I find out in the course of writing the story or book make me change elements of it or add characters.

Howard Waldrop: I'm sure all these things are somewhere in most of my stories, but I don't think I'm really conscious of them, except from a craft standpoint, i.e. story problem to solve as painlessly as possible within the narrative.

Janeen Webb: Certainly. In a collaboration, clarity is essential at the planning stage—with two authors writing, the opportunities for textual infelicities are all too real if you don't have a clear sense of direction and a checklist of character details. This does not mean that there will be no changes—writing is always an organic thing, and characters often have their own ideas about how the narrative will develop. Ongoing historical research has its own challenges: sometimes the results surprise us, sometimes we change the manuscript to accommodate new discoveries to add nuance to the storyline, sometimes we have to re-think completely. But always, the joy of discovery adds spice to the development of the counterfactual history.

Do you consciously integrate any or all of these concepts into your work and if so, how?

John Birmingham: Pretty much all the time, although I've never been forced to stop and think about how. Now that you're forcing me to do it I'm going to have to give a very personal answer. I wrote magazine journalism for ten years before I published my first book, *Felafel*, and fifteen years before *Weapons of Choice* came out. My training was in journalism, and I had some harsh instructors. Doing the research, checking sources, crosschecking sources with other sources, it was all I knew for a decade and a half of writing before

I went anywhere near alternate history. I can't help but feel this has colored my approach.

For instance, in *Without Warning* when I wanted to put my friendly pirates Jules and Fifi onto a yacht, it was not good enough to have them on board any old tub. No, they had to steal Greg Norman's yacht, didn't they? Why? Because everyone knew Greg Norman had a big yacht and, almost as importantly, the Internet was full of photographs and blueprints allowing me to faithfully recreate the experience of hijacking it, including Jules stepping in the pile of human goo that had once been The Shark. She surmised the identity of the puddle of goo because of the straw hat with the shark motif perched jauntily atop it.

The point of all this, at least as it relates to your question? The habits of fifteen years of magazine journalism were the habits I transferred across to writing alternate history. I didn't come to the genre with the list of "concepts" that you have drawn up (a pretty good list, though). I just applied the rules of writing as I knew them. Rules, incidentally, I had learned quite explicitly from the study of Tom Wolf's anthology *The New Journalism* and specifically from the introductory essay he wrote to that anthology. Folding real-world detail into a story to bury the readers inside was something I've been doing since my first published story in *Rolling Stone*.

John Crowley: I try to win over my readers by making it clear what I am up to in altering history, and make them collaborators in the enterprise—not merely to show them what a possible but not-actual history would have been like, but what it's like to think one up.

Paul Di Filippo: Given your crystallization of what were for me undefined practices, I would have to say that in my alternate history work, I've been following these precepts all along, without necessarily being able to name them until now. Principle (d) is where I think the real artistry often comes in.

William Gibson: I probably do to some extent but seldom if at all consciously.

Richard Harland: No—not even for the concepts I most agree with. The reasons why I do what I do—or did what I did—are all after-the-event for me.

Charlaine Harris: I spent some brain time figuring out if the changes I was making to societal norms of the time would be credible. After worrying about it for some time, I figured, "My world, my rules," and left it to the reader to accept those rules or not.

Christopher Priest: No.

Kim Stanley Robinson: Yes, as above.

Mary Rosenblum: I do. I constantly cross check my plot and character evolution as my research proceeds to make sure that both the plot elements and the behavior of the characters is consistent with the world I have created and its internal rules. Additionally, I plan or discard scenes depending on my research details, in order to create the most powerful sense of consistent reality that I can.

Pamela Sargent: See the above answer. I think I do integrate them more during rewrites than when I first think of a particular counterfactual idea.

Mark Shirrefs: Not consciously.

Bruce Sterling: No, I don't follow your concepts explicitly, but I agree that the narrative needs discipline. Otherwise, it becomes a silly cowboys-and-dinosaurs farrago. It's particularly easy to write bad counterhistorical fiction. The misuse of historical figures as characters in badly written fiction is particularly demeaning. It's in bad taste; it's as if the author was crassly appropriating, say, Socrates or Abraham Lincoln as puppets of his own propaganda, and this act of presumption makes a bad work even worse.

Michael Swanwick: Sometimes. Playfully.

Harry Turtledove: No, except I do keep my mind open on larger projects, knowing that things I learn later may require changes in what I've done earlier.

Janeen Webb: *The Five Star Republic* is set in the cracks of known history: the events diverge, but the society does not. So we are always conscious of the layering technique to create verisimilitude. We are also meticulous about historical research—the attention to detail pays off in so many unexpected ways.

George Zebrowski: (Regarding story worlds:) I layer the details, but then get the reader to stub his mental toe on the differences. I don't worry too much about believable or plausible, since reality can outdo it all. The name Rassmussen is misspelled in *Suns*, and when questioned about this by Poul Anderson, I told him that this was an alternate history. "Yeah, sure," he said, "that's just an excuse." But then I pointed out that the novel begins in a variant where Kennedy lived—and that this is made explicit as an end line in a middle chapter. He had not stubbed his toe as planned. Our given world engulfs us all and is hard to escape.

I do have explicit awareness of what I want to do, but I am also aware of how the material can get away from me, both well and bad, even crazy, and so I am watchful as I work, and even more so later, when the chance to meddle becomes very tempting, also to the good or bad. I work hoping for work that will get away from me, as if it were written by someone else inside me.

What might you add—or substitute—for these concepts?

John Birmingham: I haven't given the subject much thought over the years and it seems a bit late to start now, but one quite massive change to how I do these books has been obvious to me. The technology. When I set out to research *Weapons of Choice* I took myself off to a military bookstore and spent about $800 buying hardcopy works of non-fiction. When I had exhausted those I physically took myself into State library and entered the stacks. The type of research I did was not far removed from my undergraduate training. It was also slow, frustrating and frequently incomplete.

By the time I was writing the last pages in that series almost all of my research was being done online. Now I very rarely consult off-line. In the early days I found that the Internet was largely hopeless for researching general topics such as "the Battle of Midway" because to put that search string into an engine such as Google (if Google was even around back then) meant returning hundreds of thousands of very general hits. The web was pretty good for entering questions such as which brand of cigarettes did Franklin D Roosevelt smoke, but the more general the question the less useful the answer.

No longer.

I am now surrounded by a screen farm when I write. *Google*, *Wikipedia*, *Encyclopaedia Britannica*, and other much more specific reference tools run live all the time—although often hidden out of sight in one of the "virtual screens" that the Mac OS makes possible. This means that regular details such as what the weather was like on a particular day in a particular place and now available as quickly as I can type out the query. Because so much of alternate history is about the history, about the details, this is a massive change.

There is one other point I suppose I should touch on, although I wouldn't know how you would frame it as a concept. One of the enjoyable aspects of working in alternate history is using real-world characters. Sometimes, as in my *Disappearance* series those characters still very much alive, and you have to be quite careful in the way they are written. But for the *Axis of Time* series (as *Weapons of Choice* and its sequels are now known) there are a wealth of characters, both major and minor historical figures, with whom to play. We see literary novelists doing this occasionally of course, but it is much more common in our genre. There is something at work here, but I'm not sure what period for myself, I just find it great fun to write characters such as Churchill and Stalin the ensemble cast for what is effectively a great big action comic.

John Crowley: Only something like the above answer: that the creation of an alternate history ought to have a reason—why *this* alternative? It might be good entertainment to suppose that the Nazis win the Second World War and how awful that would be; but to make readers work with you to forge, and to grasp the reason for forging, a history (to forge meaning both to make and to fake) is another matter. Alternate histories have to have *more* reasons for being as they are, more significance, more human meaning, than real ones—which however have the edge of being, you, know, real.

Paul Di Filippo: I would add that the writer of alternate histories should be judicious in his choice of famous personages to incorporate into the story. Certain famous figures are in my estimation overdone by now. FDR, JFK, Mark Twain, et al—we've read enough adventures with them. Consider a book like Dick's *The Man in the High Castle*, which centers around average imaginary people. Much more authentic and challenging in its way than battening off the cheap celebrity of real people. Also, I often find that taking a real person who is not well known but who had a fascinating life opens up more territory for interstitial adventures inserted into that person's lesser-known biography.

Lisa Goldstein: As I said, I was mostly interested in the feel of the place. The Muslims in Spain were ahead of the rest of the world in terms of science, mathematics, architecture, and astronomy, and their poetry was one of the inspirations for the troubadour tradition, and I wondered what would have happened if that culture had continued. (Mostly, I thought it would be a good thing.) I tried to create a world that combined aspects of medieval Spain, Muslim culture, early industry, and science-fictional extrapolation.

Richard Harland: I suspect that the earliest, vaguest starting point for me is just a feeling for the age, a sense of atmosphere that attracts me to a particular past period. I don't mean the starting point for the story or the characters—which is something else entirely—but the starting point that makes this world into an alternate history world. Some historical periods grab my imagination—and I guess I write alternate history rather than realist historical fiction because I like to play up and intensify the flavor of that atmosphere.

I don't think you could write successful alternate history (or realist historical fiction) without a strong emotional feeling for a particular past age. No amount of research can generate it if you don't have it already—and it probably comes from somehow *inhabiting* that age through general reading or non-fictional interests or whatever. The amount of research you need to do to flesh out your world might vary enormously—not a huge amount in the case of my steampunk fantasies. My advice to aspiring steampunk authors is, do whatever research seems necessary, but don't feel obliged to devote thousands of hours to research just for the sake of it.

Charlaine Harris: I might add that you have to stick by your own rules you've made up for your world, and those rules have to make sense in terms of the action of your story. So think hard before establishing "new facts," because you're going to have to live with them.

John Kessel: See below.

Christopher Priest: See my remarks below, about *The Separation*.

Kim Stanley Robinson: For me there was an important alteration of the Shippey ideas quoted below: the change point in history, for me, should illustrate some historical principle, some theory of history; and also, the way I put it is this: it should be the largest possibly historical change that can still be well compared to our own real history. Thus, Harry Harrison in *East of Eden* (?) told about a world in which dinosaurs survived and rose to intelligence and stayed on Earth into our time, but this is something too big to be usefully compared to our history, so it is not really working as an alternative history. It goes too far. You want a comparison always going on, between what really happened and the changed history's events. So: I will declare that my *Years of Rice and Salt* change (which is that all the Europeans die in the Black Death) is the Largest Possible Change that the alternative history can handle!! That's why I quit doing them when I was done with that.

Mary Rosenblum: Too often, what I see in historical fiction is a carefully crafted world with a character mindset or world view that is far too modern for the world that the author has created. We all want our readers to identify with people who are like us, but that does thin out the integrity of the world being created, in my opinion. It is very difficult, granted, to create a character whose world view may seem less than positive to readers, but when it is achieved, in historical or alternate history fiction, it really enriches the sense of "other time."

Pamela Sargent: That plausibility is essential (that is, in a work of alternate or counterfactual historical fiction; I'd allow more latitude for the related form of historical fantasy) and being gratuitous (assuming that, to cite an obvious sort of example, a B-1 bomber suddenly shows up to help the losing side win an important historical battle) is to be avoided. Okay, you can insert a B-1 bomber in a time travel story that deals with that important historical battle, but I draw a distinction between time travel stories and alternate history stories. (I know there can sometimes be an overlap between the two.)

Mark Shirrefs: Gut instinct. An idea feels right or wrong. Analysis of why may or may not be necessary depending on the circumstances, e.g. if I have to explain to someone less experienced with story construction.

Bruce Sterling: I like writing counterfactual history about other people's histories—counterfactual versions of cultures that are not my own. If I were to write about, say, contemporary Surinam, a Surinamese might take that rather ill. An alien always makes beginners' mistakes, and that might seem appropriative.

But if I were to write about, say, an alternative super-Surinam that's bigger than Brazil, a local might welcome that and appreciate the study involved. People are commonly touched when you show an extensive interest in their own history. Commonly they don't know much about their history themselves. This can be construed as a generous and sympathetic act by a foreign author, while simply writing about contemporary Surinam might be perceived as stealing their clothes. It interests me to see counter-historical fiction touching areas of discourse that are closed to other forms of fiction.

Michael Swanwick: An awareness of what history the reader might reasonably be expected to know. If a story hinges on George Washington becoming a British general, that fact would not need much exposition. If its jonbar point is that Nicola Tesla stayed with Edison's laboratory rather than defecting to George Westinghouse, a great deal more work will be required to make it clear that this did not happen in our own history and why it is a significant enough moment to radically change history.

General reactions, negative or positive?

Paul Di Filippo: I think these guidelines should be taught at all SF writing workshops!

William Gibson: Feels reductive, in terms of what might actually be done. The thing I find most off-putting about "genre" is its exclusionary sense. M. John Harrison recently remarked that the first rule of Genre Club was that you have to be doing it for whatever reasons Genre Club assumes it's done for, and if you aren't, even though you do it, you aren't doing it. I think you may be defining the way Genre Club says alternate history must be done in order to be it.

The record of alternative historical fiction is largely one of remarkably poorly written novels, to my taste at least. The good ones really do stand out. It's as if the form itself can be a remarkably efficient recipe for bad novels. I think this is a result of a certain unusually reductive sense of what novels "are for."

Richard Harland: My general reaction is to say that alternative history in my steampunk fantasies is more of a means than an end. That is, it's a way of placing an imaginary world in relation to our own real world rather than a categorization of the body of the novel itself. By analogy, an SF trope such as space travel or time travel can be used as a means of transporting the protagonist(s) to a world that isn't SF in spirit at all, e.g. a planet of primitive warfare in the style of epic fantasy. Would you describe such a novel as SF? I'd say that it's epic fantasy at heart, but with a "real-connection" in SF mode. In the same way, my juggernaut novels are steampunk fantasy at heart—or *Song of the Slums* is gaslight romance at heart (as a sub-section of steampunk)—but they link to reality in the mode of alternate history. I've always believed that genre shouldn't be an exclusive either-or way to categorize fiction.

I don't think this rules me out of this discussion, though—it only locates me in a specific territory of alternate history writing. I've argued elsewhere that steampunk has a *natural* affinity with alternate history. Epic or traditional fantasy tends most often to a simple otherworld setting, but otherworlds don't suit steampunk nearly as well. I'll quote myself:

For much traditional fantasy, real-connection exists only in the form of disconnection; the reader is presented with a simple otherworld that bears no visible relation to our own real world. George R. R. Martin's *A Game of Thrones* in his *A Song of Ice and Fire* series provides a topical example. This is a much more difficult gambit for steampunk authors. It's not implausible that any relatively early society might have evolved such cultural features as, say, swords, wine, saddles or castles—after all, many different societies on our own planet have managed to do so. But when we move into the First Industrial Age of the nineteenth century, the cultural features become much more specialized. Can we really believe that an unrelated otherworld might just *happen* to evolve umbrellas, bustles, top hats and doilies? It's simpler to posit a world that is partly the real nineteenth century, but with certain divergences. And, by fortunate coincidence, alternate history as a genre possibility quite apart from steampunk rises to prominence in the same period or a little earlier—as witness Phillip

K. Dick's seminal classic, *The Man in the High Castle,* published in 1962. There are steampunk worlds that are also otherworlds (e.g. Stephen Hunt's *Jackelian* series starting with *The Court of the Air*), as there are steampunk worlds that are also retro-futures (e.g. Phillip Reeve's *Mortal Engines* and its sequels), but the alternate history form of real-connection is overall the most popular (e.g. Gibson & Sterling's *The Difference Engine,* Cherie Priest's *Boneshaker*).

(That's from a critical anthology on steampunk not yet published.)

Christopher Priest: Negative, I fear.

Kim Stanley Robinson: Seems like you are on a good track here.

Mark Shirrefs: Positive.

Bruce Sterling: I'm all for formulating concepts. They don't have to be correct to be genuinely useful to writers. For instance, if "Counterfactual fiction is defined by its relation to history," then what does fiction look like when it disobeys that rule? I'd be guessing that it looks like historical romance fiction, where the female lead surely finds her One True Love whether it's Regency England or Pharaonic Egypt.

Or what if it's "bitterly antagonistic" relation to history? That might be a school of national revanchist counterfactual fiction, where, say, the South wins the Civil War again and again, for whole sets of different reasons, all intended to put the boot into the damn Yankees. Literary concepts can be fruitful when correct or mistaken.

Michael Swanwick: While alternate history is an identifiable form, it is not a difficult one to comprehend or to write. The best model here would be Columbus's egg. (I'll presume you know the story.) Once it's been done, and the trick has been seen, it's easily reproducible by any skilled writer.

Harry Turtledove: As with anything else, doing a lot of A-H makes doing it easier. Your mind gets its equivalent of muscle memory, knowing how something is supposed to work and finding a way to put it across.

#

Earlier, I quoted Tom Shippey's "divergent point rule," i.e., that a divergence point in a counterfactual fiction should be (1) plausible, (2) definite, (3) small in itself, and (4) massive in consequence"). What do you think?

John Crowley: It's a good rule, though I could not have formulated it myself, I think I followed it in a time-travel story called *Great Work of Time*, which created an imaginary British empire that continues to flourish after the one we know has declined and vanished. The turning-point there was the death of the imperialist and diamond entrepreneur Cecil Rhodes: if he dies in a certain period his fortune is given to a secret society to further and preserve the Empire. Since the secret society eventually comes to be in possession of a means of time travel, it is able to return to Africa and cause the death of Rhodes, thus bringing itself and its works into being.

Charlaine Harris: That makes a lot of sense to me. My divergence point (the assassination) could certainly have turned out the way it did, and the American government could have toppled in consequence. The death of one man can make an enormous difference to the decades following.

Mark Shirrefs: I'm not sure about Tom's third point. A divergence point might not necessarily be small, for example the Axis forces winning the Second World War in *The Man in the High Castle*.

Tom's third point might work the other way too—that is, a massive event brings about a small consequence—although that consequence might be massive in terms of the story you are creating.

For example, in the recent *War of the Worlds* movie with Tom Cruise, Martians invade the Earth, but unlike other stories where it's the defeat of the aliens that is the main narrative, here it's about the improvement of Tom's character's relationship with his family. So, a massive event—the invasion—causes a small consequence—a man gets on better with his kids.

Harry Turtledove: "Small in itself" I would disagree with. Aliens invading in the Second World War, time-traveling South Africans with AK-47s, a different planet in the fourth orbit of the solar system, a world where Gibraltar never reopened ... those aren't small changes. "Massive in consequence" for whom, and to what degree? I've written a piece—"The House That George Built" on *Tor.com*—where the consequences of Milwaukee rather than

Baltimore getting a Federal League franchise in 1914 were massive for Babe Ruth, but not for the world at large. 1 and 2 seem pretty much inarguable.

Janeen Webb: I do not believe counterfactual fiction must necessarily have a single divergence point: in my own case, there are a number of tiny divergences that occur in response to known circumstances, and, collectively, these add up to produce a significant change in political, scientific and social direction. That said, I do agree that the divergences that create counterfactual history should be plausible and definite. If you get that right, they will be massive in consequence. The first question I always ask is: "what's at stake?"

Are you conscious of any such "rules" when you're writing alternate history?

Terry Bisson: As you can see, alternate history (for me) follows certain rules, and yes I am so imbedded in them that I need not be conscious of them.

Paul Di Filippo: I'm not so much a fan of "small in itself." That would rule out all those "Nazis won World War Two" books, which, while now somewhat clichéd, still offered some thrills when fresh. It seems to me that a big divergence point—Harry Harrison's intelligence arising in dinosaurs in *West of Eden*—can lead to wonderful books.

William Gibson: As a reader, I am aware of the pleasure of reading an alternate historical novel (say Amis' superb *The Alteration*) which perfectly obeys its own rules. Except when it very deliberately sneaks a little too close to breaking its own rules, which provides another kind of pleasure entirely. And I am aware of the equally great pleasure provided by a work like Ned Bauman's *The Teleportation Accident*, in which dashing young German bohemians attend ketamine parties in 1930s Berlin, no explanation whatever in the "genre" sense. These are related literary pleasures, it seems to me, but I don't have a framework in which I can explicate the experience.

Richard Harland: For "rules," the same answer as before! But I fully endorse Shippey's (3) and (4)—there's something intrinsically appealing about a POD that's small in itself but massive in consequences. I don't know exactly what he means by "plausible," but for myself, I'm often attracted to a POD that's historically justified but at first sight *implausible*. For example, Albert Favier-Mathieu's plan to dig a tunnel under the English Channel. I love the quirky bits of history, the oddities that never came to fruition or fell rapidly by the wayside. Probably most steampunk writers feel this fascination!

But maybe Shippey gives a more specialized meaning to "plausible" ...

Charlaine Harris: Certainly. I think you have to anchor your narrative firmly in what really happened so your alternate reality will ring true to the reader.

John Kessel: To some degree, yes. I want the counterfactual to illuminate some element of real history. I want it to make a comment on history, or the real people it is about, or about some element of human nature that applies to the real world.

Christopher Priest: In the second part of your questionnaire you have three questions about rules. I didn't become a writer so that I could invent rules or follow the rules of others. The moment I hear about a rule I either ignore it or look for a way to subvert it. I haven't read the Shippey essay you're quoting, but if I did my immediate instinct would be to try to subvert it.

Kim Stanley Robinson: Yes, as above, but I don't think the change has to be too small in itself, obviously. That would be to get stuck in the "for want of a nail the shoe was lost" theory of history, which is not the only one. Asimov in *The End of Eternity* seemed to postulate that history had a kind of "reversion to the mean" tropism or tendency, so that you could change some things in history but it would tend to try to get back to the "big flow" of some kind of deterministic flow. That would suggest you need some very big changes to make any differences. It's almost a reverse Shippey, and you should consider that kind of story too.

Mary Rosenblum: Absolutely! A divergent point is useless if readers don't have a clue what actually happened or how this story differs from what actually happened. Thus, a divergent point needs to effect a change that even the average reader with today's minimal grasp of history can recognize. And the cascade of alternate events leading from that divergence point needs to be extensive enough to allow for a novel's worth or a series' worth of plot. In the case of my own alternate history America, the landing of the Chinese on the continent and the introduction of small pox and a crude vaccine for the disease permitted the indigenous Americans to maintain their populations without the ravages of disease that actually occurred, and to have achieved gunpowder and developed gunpowder weapons before the Europeans landed. This permitted a far-reaching cascade of changes that affect the entire US history from the first contact.

The actual divergence point was when China continued its naval dominance and explorations rather than withdrawing into the continent as it did, enabling it to establish permanent settlements on the American continents and exist as a naval power during European explorations. But too few readers would recognize this divergence point, so I used a world post-European invasion, which all readers would recognize as "different" and quickly understand why it was different.

Pamela Sargent: Plausibility, yes. Small in itself? I'm not so sure. What counts as a small change? The death of one person, any person, is a "small" change in the world, given that we're all going to die, but it makes a difference whether that person is, say, a homeless man or President John F. Kennedy. The death of a butterfly is inconsequential unless it happens in Ray Bradbury's "A Sound of Thunder."

Mark Shirrefs: No.

Bruce Sterling: I'm conscious of the rule that it's a good idea not to make the reader suffer for my homework. I believe that my works of counter-historical fiction should necessarily be a subset of my own widened historical understanding. One needs to know much more history than appears on the page, and to know history, I think it's necessary to demonstrate some respect for generational experience and driving historical forces.

Lewis Shiner and I wrote a short story, "Mozart in Mirrorshades," where imperialist time travelers show grave disrespect for the past. These marauders really don't care what was important or what was going on in the past, they're just there to loot and exploit mankind's heritage for their own petty benefit. The effect of this on the reader is quite painful, in an interesting way.

Michael Swanwick: There are no rules. Or, rather, there used to be rules before Howard Waldrop wrote "Ike at the Mike," in which hearing a snatch of live music causes the young Dwight D. Eisenhower to abandon his plans for a military career in order to become a jazz musician. This is implausible to an extreme. You could argue that by Shippey's rule "Ike at the Mike" is not a good alternate history story. Yet it's a good story, it's alternate history, and without invoking the rule there's no way of denying that it's a good alternate history story.

Before Waldrop did a violence to the concept of alternate history, it was a donnish form based on deep readings into history. In his wake, we've had an explosion of implausible alternate histories, most absurdly *Saturday Night Live*'s "What If—?" skits, answering such questions as "What if Napoleon had a B-52 at the Battle of Waterloo?" and "What if Eleanor Roosevelt could fly?"

Harry Turtledove: Not really, but I always have been very much a seat-of-the-pants writer.

Howard Waldrop: In "Calling Your Name" in the Janis Ian-edited *Stars* I wrote a truly personal alternate history, i.e. the whole world has changed, and it doesn't make a damn bit of difference to anyone but the protagonist. (Read a reprinted version somewhere, as the first printing of the story in *Stars* was the only one that was screwed up—not changed from the typed-up copy-edited version …) But mostly, none of this is conscious, except as a story problem, i.e. what would a world that had changed mean to someone who wasn't the protagonist? (Like his wife and daughters and neighbors and the public at large.)

Janeen Webb: I really don't think you can apply any hard and fast rules to writing counterfactual history (or anything else, for that matter). I think of them as guidelines. I'm conscious of keeping to the planning decisions about narrative voice, historical detail and so on that inform the structure of the book. After that, no. The writing process itself has its own logic, and that isn't bound by rules.

George Zebrowski: As long as we live in a creative universe (proven so by Kurt Gödel), fiction cannot be inspired by rules; it can only be discovered, stumbled into, guessed at. Of course, mechanical fiction can be produced, to its own detriment. Sounds a lot like reality.

If you believe alternate history to be rule-generated, what rules do you follow?

Paul Di Filippo: Insofar as history is a "hard science," one should attempt to understand developmental principles of culture, economics, politics, etc. which can be deduced from study of our consensus history and then applied to the imaginary creations.

Lisa Goldstein: I do believe there should be a divergence point. I've read alternate history where the changes are all over the place, and it isn't terribly believable. That's the only rule I follow, though.

Charlaine Harris: You have to choose the changes you make to history wisely. For the occasional reader who actually researches the point of time in history you jump off of, there has to be enough there to cause them to feel your version could have happened.

John Kessel: One rule that I follow that a lot of alternate histories do not, and that to me undermines such stories, is that *if one is writing about an alternative career for someone who in our world became known in one area, the new career or arc of that person's life should arise out of known facts of the real person's history and capacities.*

Howard Waldrop's "Ike at the Mike" has been celebrated; it depicts an alternate history where Elvis Presley, instead of being the first white rock and roll artist, becomes a senator, and Dwight Eisenhower, instead of becoming a military leader and president, is a jazz musician. This story has always bothered me. As far as I know, Elvis had little interest in or capacity for politics, and Eisenhower had absolutely no musical ability. The story trades on the novelty of imagining these people in what seem to us very surprising careers, but it is in my opinion completely bogus.

There are a host of such stories, and I find them all very annoying. Making Martin Luther King the point guard for the 1957 Celtics does not tell us anything about history, or about basketball, or about Martin Luther King. It's a conceit, essentially a joke, not an illumination.

When I put George H. W. Bush and Fidel Castro into baseball careers in my story "The Franchise," I based this on the fact that

Bush was the captain of the Yale baseball team that went to the college world series in 1948, and Castro was a skilled pitcher and (by some reports, which I later found may be inaccurate but which I read when I got the idea for the story) was scouted by the New York Giants.

I suppose it's possible to drop a character into the background in a bizarrely different role than we know as a little joke, without doing damage to the concept or credibility. I think Michael Moorcock wrote an alternate history where there is a British bobby patrolling the London streets named Michael Jagger. But I'm wary of placing such a joke at the center of the story.

Kim Stanley Robinson: History itself has no very good rules, because we don't have any counter-examples, so I don't tend to think of it as a matter of "rules." I like to feel I know what the story idea's theory of history is, and then test that theory. *Can* one person make a difference? I tend to ask questions, and then just see what the story idea makes me write. It's very intuitive, along with being rational and historical informed. For *Years* I definitely read a lot of global world histories, and historiographies.

Mary Rosenblum: The only rule that I recognize in fiction, in writing in general, is that it must work. That is, the effect on the readers needs to be the effect that the writer intends. That can be effected in many many ways, but usually, by achieving that balance, in fiction at least, of world, character, and plot elements.

Pamela Sargent: If I have any rule for anything, including the writing of alternate history, it's always to remember that anything that happens in this world is contingent. It might not have happened that way. It might not have happened at all. Something else entirely might have happened instead. Never think of anything as inevitable. This obviously doesn't mean anything can happen, but I fail to see how a fatalist would approach alternate history.

At the same time, there is an inertia to history that resists even a cascade of divergent points or significant changes. For example, one of the two principal political parties in the United States now basically supports the notion that a society owes little or nothing to its poorest citizens, not even a guarantee of access to needed medical care. This is not a position that suddenly appeared out of nowhere; this is the same party that fiercely resisted the New Deal reforms of Franklin Delano Roosevelt in the 1930s. There is a strong, individualistic and paranoid style of American politics likely to persist for historical and sociological reasons even if more progressive forces make gains/ create points of divergence. Incidents like the 9/11 attacks and the administration of George W. Bush might have accelerated the rise of more regressive political movements in the United States, but the potential for their rise was always present.

Bruce Sterling: I think that the voice of the past is important. I try to read a lot of contemporary work from the period of study. Verbal parody and mimicry is very useful. Period slang is also of great interest. If you want to talk about the past, listen first. They were people like you are, they're not your ideological tinker toys.

Michael Swanwick: Obviously, I don't. If I did, I'd say they're (1) Be entertaining, and (2) If absolutely necessary, ignore Rule 1.

Harry Turtledove: I believe alternate history, like any other fiction, is character—or story-generated. Rules beyond telling an interesting, thought-provoking story are just silly.

Howard Waldrop: I have only one rule which I follow in *all* my alternate histories (and elsewhere).

A person (historical) has to be born when and where they were (in our world.) They may live longer and have a different life or some crux point, but that's life.

In my story "The Horse of a Different Color (That You Rode in On)" I have Manfred Marx (the oldest Marx Bros.) live to be 107, and have a career in vaudeville, radio and TV as a solo, then duo act. In real life he died at the age of six months in a diphtheria epidemic. No reason, etc. for virulent disease, his life couldn't have become true. (The story *isn't* alt. history—its concerns are elsewhere.)

In "A Better World's in Birth" I have Richard Wagner rise to become head of a Revolutionary United States of Europe in the 1850s, because during the Revolutions of 1848–9, after taking his wife to Chemnitz, he returned to Dresden and did not, as in our world, return to Chemnitz and take up the life of a fugitive in Switzerland. It *could* have happened that way. A matter of *not* turning around.

What rules come to mind as being important from your practitioner's perspective?

Terry Bisson: I like Shippey's rules except for #3. The divergence point can be "small" (a plane crash in Stan Robinson's "The Lucky Strike" or huge (who won the war) in *Man in the High Castle*. Dick could have gone small (no break in the clouds before the Battle of Midway) but wasn't interested in the war itself.

John Crowley: I can't really think of any rules that would cover all the possibilities. Philip Dick's *Man in the High Castle* (which is I suppose one candidate for original AH novel) works on different principles (or rules) from the apparently similar *SS-GB* of Len Deighton. The only rule I can think that applies universally also applies to all other fiction: you can get away with anything you can get away with.

Paul Di Filippo: Try to avoid the bad practice identified in the Turkey City Lexicon as "I suffered for my research and now the reader will too!"

Richard Harland: The only rule I'd want to hold consciously in mind is the general rule for all imaginative fiction: whatever you imagine, *follow through on it*. Be aware that a shift away from reality (including real history) in one place is going to have consequences in other places.

Charlaine Harris: Believability. Your world must ring true. That's partly up to the decision the writer makes when forming a new world, and partly up to skill on the part of the writer.

John Kessel: Another rule I would suggest is that, *once you make a significant change in history as we know it, you must take account for the fact that such a change, if it is a large one, will alter all the history afterward, and so many of the people and events and institutions and a host of other things that exist in our history will not exist in this alternate history.* If you have the South win the Civil War, then you can't reasonably have Louis Armstrong playing jazz cornet in 1930, or the same course of history in, say, the First World War or the Second World War. Those wars probably won't even happen, or if they do they take profoundly different course. Many people who are born in our history are never born, and others are born who never were in our history. Etc.

Kim Stanley Robinson's *The Years of Rice and Salt* deals with this element fairly, as so many alternate histories do not. Once most of the population of Europe is wiped out by the Black Plague, many of the historical figures we know never come to exist, and the course of colonialism, politics, invention, science, the arts, and a hundred other things is vastly different.

Kim Stanley Robinson: Hayden White's book (title forgotten?)[1] shows how all the great historiographers of the nineteenth century actually were applying very simplistic narrative schemes from literature to world history itself. Thus the big historians were doing either tragedy or comedy, etc. etc. I will have to find that reference for you, because it is a crucial text for understanding what alternative histories are doing, I think.

It helps to read philosophy of history when doing this work, because you get to this realization, like William Goldman about Hollywood: no one knows anything. This is both daunting and liberating. Whatever you do in alternative history, no one can say to you: "That's just wrong." People *do* say that in reviews, of course, and all too frequently, but they are the ones who are wrong. Real history is contingent and full of bizarre accidents. It can't be predicted and can barely be written at all. My impression is that there is a crisis in the theory of history, brought about by the close examinations of Theory, especially postmodern deconstructionism; there is no good working historical method, all history is a fiction, and as such, maybe it's always an "alternative history" being written, because it never corresponds to whatever really happened. So I liked to keep that stuff in mind when I was doing alternative history.

Mary Rosenblum: The world needs to be a character, that is, it is not sufficient to use it as a painted backdrop on which a story plays out that could play out in Omaha or London. The world itself needs to have power and influence on the other elements of the story. Otherwise, it is nothing more than a backdrop.

---

[1] I found the Hayden White book which is called *Metahistory* and is copyright dated 1973. Its epigraph is from Bachelard's *Psychology of Fire*: "One can study only what one has first dreamed about." Sounds like you are my friend.

Pamela Sargent: The point of divergence might be small, but shouldn't be trivial.

Mark Shirrefs: "Plausibility" is absolutely necessary and I spend a lot of time making sure this is maintained.

There's also the issue of consistency, or making sure you stick to the rules of the world you have created. If these rules are not the rules of the world with which the audience is familiar, it's vital to scrutinize every aspect of the story from the perspective of these rules and make sure they're consistent.

Bruce Sterling: "The past is a kind of future that already happened."

Michael Swanwick: Speaking only for my own work, not anybody else's, I feel strongly that the deviance from actual history should be both colorful and comprehensible to the reader. As familiarity with history declines not only in America but around the world, this last becomes increasingly more difficult to achieve.

Harry Turtledove: Thou shalt not bore the reader.

#

And lastly (and perhaps most importantly) ...

What devices, techniques, and processes do *you* employ to create alternate histories? (For instance, do you use timelines, inventions such as time machines, quotes, or any other devices to create plausibility?)

Terry Bison: One device you didn't mention, which turns up in my *Fire on the Mountain* and Dick's *Man in the High Castle*, (and probably others as well) is the appearance of a "fictional" book about or elements of the Actual World (the one we live in) which people find preposterous or even disgusting. Lafferty's "The Interurban Queen" (alt. world without cars and highways) does this brilliantly with crazy outlaws who drive cars. People shoot them from trains for sport).

John Crowley: See above. I've used a time machine. I understand generally the chronology of my stories set in the past (altered or not) but I don't write time lines (or outlines either).

Paul Di Filippo: For me, the forking infinite multiverse is such a given. I don't generally find it necessary to explain the reality of an alternate timeline. Just jump into it.

Richard Harland: Since I start with a world existing at a distance from the real world/real history, my effort is always to create plausibility backwards, i.e. how the world that we know from real history might have got itself into this very different state. I always write out careful timelines, just like any serious historian—especially because my steampunk history involves not one but a whole succession of changes over an extended timeframe.

Maybe this is the moment to say what's been at the back of my mind all along. My use of alternate history lets me swing a long way away from the world we know because it allows for developments over decades. And once you've gone beyond a single first change, history can throw up any number of unexpected twists and turns. For example, my POD of a tunnel under the English Channel leading to an invasion of England ... the obvious extension here would be that the Napoleonic Empire triumphs and at least some of the principles of the French Revolution influence all subsequent history? Not so in my steampunk history. On the contrary, the invasion is thwarted, the French army driven back, and the Napoleonic Wars continue on for thirty years longer than in real history. But *that* has its own consequences—and very big consequences they are!

I guess I'm skeptical about historical prediction and one-track theories of history. I don't believe that history operates in straight lines—rather, it's full of switchback turns and unfoldings. The one thing we can be sure of is that any change will end up changing the dimensions of the way people think. And once you've posited one change, who knows what changes-upon-changes-upon-changes might follow?

The way I "play" with alternate history is almost like one of those word-puzzles where you have to go by stages from one word to some other wholly different word—altering one letter at a time and producing a valid dictionary word at each stage. That's me—moving from one state of society to another wholly different state of society by way of successive in-between stages, each of which has to evolve naturally from the preceding stage and make perfect, plausible sense in itself. I can end up traversing a lot of ground like that!

Charlaine Harris: I am not an organized writer, I'm ashamed to say. I do have a notebook full of information I looked up that I felt would be useful, and most of it has been ... if only it were better organized! From the time San Simeon was built to the dates of the births of Nicholas's children to the development of public parks in San Diego to the time when refrigerators were common in American homes ... you just never know what you will need. I'm constantly surprised by what I need to look up.

Kim Stanley Robinson: No time machines, yikes, that would be a different genre! Alternative history is *real* and does not get into parallel worlds or travel between alternate timelines. That would be a different genre.

I did use timelines for *Years*, just to keep track of where I was. Each century's developments would then constrain what I could imagine for the next chapter.

Plausibility is a matter of details, and realism in literary terms, what Barthes calls "the effect of the real" (extraneous details that are there anyway), etc.

Mary Rosenblum: I look for divergence points that open up a wealth of possibilities, both social and historical, and that can be explored on multiple levels. I also look for historical periods where I can realistically find the details necessary to weave a seemingly complete fabric for the readers. Not all historical periods are easily researched even if they have fascinating potential, and it would be difficult to create a real and in depth world. Not every divergence is one that most readers will recognize. The divergence either needs to lead to societal changes that make the divergence clear (my Aboriginal America for example) or directly affect an historical event that makes the divergence clear to readers (John Kennedy is not shot).

I have seen "excerpts" from "history books" used at the start of each chapter to bring readers up to speed on what is happening and that can be effective with a certain type of story, but it's not a technique I've used.

Pamela Sargent: I think the best way to answer this is to discuss the writing of my own alternate historical fiction. My story "The Sleeping Serpent" began with a what-if question that grew out of research I did for my historical novel *Ruler of the Sky*: What if the Mongols had conquered all of Europe instead of turning back in 1241 (when, after the death of the Great Khan Ogedei, they returned to Mongolia to elect a successor)? That was the initial assumption, but I also had the notion of writing something set in a familiar landscape (the regions of New York City and the Hudson River) and with Mohawk/Iroquois characters. I had also been reading some captivity narratives about early European settlers who had been captured by Native Americans and made lives for themselves among the Indians. (Mary Jemison, one of these captives, is still honored as an ancestor by her Seneca descendants.) This is where inspiration for a particular story can escape any rules for the writing of the story; I thought it would be cool to have Mohawks and Mongols in the same story, as both peoples were formidable warriors, and the only way to do that was in an alternate history that assumed a Mongol conquest of Europe and a subsequent Mongol discovery of North and South America. Other assumptions branched off from that; I assumed the Mongols hadn't conquered England (for much the same reasons they failed in a naval invasion of Japan) and that both English (Inglistani) settlers and the Mongols were contending for control of what we know as New York and New England. My central characters were a Mongol man who was captured by Mohawks as a child and grew up among them before returning to his own people, and a minor son of a European Khan who had been sent to oversee the Mongol encampment on Manhattan Island. How do I create plausibility? Looking back, the only answer that makes sense is that I begin with an assumption that is at least plausible (what if the Mongols had conquered all of Europe?) and then see what can plausibly follow from that. I don't know how useful that is as a device for other writers, as much of the process is unconscious, or at least semiconscious, for me.

Bruce Sterling: Yes, I do have timelines. I use biographies of major characters, and I often use a "mood board" of contemporary images: the clothing, architecture, important period figures, publications, art movements, and so on. Sometimes I play period music while writing.

Michael Swanwick: Bald-faced chutzpah. If the story obviously believes in itself, the reader will too.

Harry Turtledove: I've used quotes, I've used imaginary newspaper and magazine pieces, I've certainly used a time machine—whatever I need to get things across to the reader.

Howard Waldrop: I'm a great believer in *cumulative* hinge points, rather than one great "Saul on the way to Tarsus" event that changes everything forever.

I've been doing this so long I've used (or *we've* used, when I collaborated with others—mostly Utley[2]) about every way of doing it there is—narrative, documents, hidden connections, sheer dumb luck, a piece of unrelated knowledge from research from *another* story—to get the job done

I use as many techniques as each story requires. Sometimes you can do it as straight narrative (hard without info-dumps, but possible, sometimes with documents, films, TV shows, etc. (the "layering" you talk about.) Anything to convince the reader you know what you're talking about. No matter how left-field it seems at first, if you do your job you can convince the reader (*and* the characters) it's right.

The Moone World (in progress): to make the 1835 Moon Hoax be true, I had to f*** with the physics of the Solar System. The Moon has to be almost a twin-earth, be further from Earth etc. to have an atmosphere and support life to cover its orbit in 28.2 days. It has to move faster etc. Why not? So that was the operative deep idea behind *The Moone World*. All these things would have no effect on Earth, until man tried to *go there*. Huge changes, little notice.

In "Hoover's Men" (above, among other things, rapid development in TV technology in the 1920s), I had regular programming like in the 1950s starting in the 1930s. The retired Radio Police-man is watching Gable and Lombard in same sitcom they did. This is a coda to the actual story itself.

Janeen Webb: One of the most important choices a writer must make at planning stage is the narrative voice of the tale. It's not just a question of deciding on point of view: the narrative voice determines a whole raft of important stylistic elements. In *The Five Star Republic*, we chose the narrative voice of a progressive C19th novelist to make it *feel* like the novel was contemporary with the counterfactual events. That's not to say the voice is an

---

[2]Steven Utley (1948–2013).

exact copy—no modern reader would sit still for the convolutions of C19th grammar and syntax. I learned that lesson writing a short story, "Manifest Destiny," for Gillian Polack's original anthology, *Baggage*. I did write that story in pure C19th century form, only to be told "love it, can't publish it. Please re-write."

In terms of narrative process, *because* we are writing counterfactual history we check every detail: we are strict about language—we don't allow words that weren't in use at the time, or weren't invented yet. Our characters use period expressions, and we employ slightly old-fashioned grammar, but sparingly. We also adhere to the sometimes awkward social conventions of the time, which gives a sense of period-appropriate formality without slowing the action.

We are also sticklers for period-appropriate technology. Everything we include was invented or in development at the time. Our narrative tweaks are confined to building on what was perfectly possible if political, economic or personal circumstances had been just that little bit different.

How do you come up with ideas for alternate history?

Andrew Enstice: At this point it might be worth pointing out a common characteristic of history and counterfactual history: they are both histories—stories constructed by a creative combination of available evidence and extrapolation. In the case of what became our historical starting-point, a gold miners' rebellion against British authorities in the Australian colony of Victoria, the generally accepted historical narrative has been shaped initially by a single eye-witness account, later extended by reminiscences of some of those who took part. Subsequent historians have contented themselves with adding to, amplifying or amending this foundational narrative.

Janeen Webb and I came to the whole affair without that preconception, instead looking for other, neglected points of view. And found that whole sections of the narrative were based on downplaying or ignoring evidence already in the public domain. (To such an extent that we were able to use our fiction to present findings of fact overlooked by generations of historians who had not considered it worthwhile to follow such trails.) The history, in other words, was highly selective.

We reinserted some of those neglected elements and characters. And foregrounded a subsequent real turning-point event—the 1873 global stock market crash, which severely weakened the British Empire and created a plausible space for counterfactual constitutional and economic reform in Australia. Add a consequent investment in John Ericsson's nascent solar steam technology, and the solar-powered *Five Star Republic* becomes a completely plausible alternative to disastrously polluting industry in the late nineteenth and twentieth centuries.

John Crowley: Who hasn't dreamed of a world other than the one we live in? Better, sweeter, fairer? Worse? I think often of such things, and about canceling the worst of the past: World War One being a prime example. Any history I read makes me propose alternative versions, or wish I could have been at this juncture or that to make everything different. If I could turn every alternate world I have thought of into a novel, I'd have quite a shelf—and if coming up with a great idea was the hard part of making a book I might.

Paul Di Filippo: I think the best such stories arise from creating a world the author would like to at least explore or even inhabit. An upcoming project of mine is to do a novel which diverges circa 1910, in which the entire awful twentieth century never happens—at least not as we know it did.

William Gibson: I tend to meditate on the difficulty of imagining the subjective experience of the world prior to audio recording. I have no idea why, but this seldom fails to open things up. If nothing else it reminds me that the course of history was stranger, bigger, more complex, less known, than any fantasy of mine.

Lisa Goldstein: There are a lot of places where it would be fascinating to see what would have happened if history had turned out differently. One of the great tragedies of the world for me was the burning of the Library of Alexandria, and I wonder what the world would be like now if we still had all those books. This has a place in a novel I just finished, not alternate history but time travel, where my characters get to go back and visit the Library. One of the best parts of writing this part was that I got to read a lot about that time.

Richard Harland: It helps to know plenty of real history, and real history has been a hobby of mine for as long as I can remember. I don't mean the history of any one period, but *all* of history—suggesting parallels from quite different times and places. For example, the attempted right-wing revolution/coup in *Song of the Slums* grew from the fact that I'd just ended the Fifty Years War, so obviously there were going to be a lot of returning ex-soldiers. Also obviously, they weren't going to be pleased with a peace-without-victory that produced no benefits for them, and in fact left them unemployed and unemployable. The parallel that sprang to mind was the aftermath of the First World War—with the attempted right-wing putsches in Germany and elsewhere—especially Mussolini's March on Rome, which led to the Fascist dictatorship in Italy. The conditions in my world were ripe for exactly the same kind of development: dissatisfied ex-soldiers and various right-wing powers that could harness that dissatisfaction to their own ends.

Charlaine Harris: If you can write fiction, you can write alternate history. It's just history with different decorations.

John Kessel: I don't seek them out; they present themselves to me.

Kim Stanley Robinson: They came to me as visions. For a while I was hunting for them. "Vinland the Dream" I found by thinking about how small the evidences for the reality of the Vinland story really were; so small that it suddenly seemed the whole thing could have been a hoax.

Mary Rosenblum: A simple application of "what if" to everything I read.

Pamela Sargent: I've always been interested in history and was lucky enough to have very good history teachers in both secondary school and college. To come up with good ideas for alternate history requires an interest in history, but also an interest in almost everything—the history of science, technological developments, different cultures, anthropology, engineering—you name it. The more areas you explore and the more you try to learn about everything, even small things, the more plausible and convincing any alternate history is likely to be. For example, a good case can be made that any Mongol conquest of western Europe was unlikely even if Ogedei hadn't died in 1241 (forests instead of steppes to fight in, a more humid climate that might damage Mongol bows and other weapons, etc.) so I had to assume that the invading Mongols would be as inventive in mastering new weapons and ways of fighting, making allies of those who might otherwise be enemies, and as ruthless as they had been in China and Central Asia. This is a roundabout way of saying that the writer always has to know and be aware of a lot more than the reader, one way to get at the "layering" you mentioned earlier.

Mark Shirrefs: The *Spellbinder* TV series involved traveling to a parallel Earth where magic seemed to exist. It wasn't really magic but a very advanced technology (thanks Arthur C. Clarke).

My writing partner and I needed a reason why this technology existed so we started doing research on magnetic control of energy, which led us to Tesla's work on broadcast energy and to speculations about what the world would be like if we relied on magnetism for power generation instead of fossil fuel.

Our divergence point for the *Spellbinder* story was that once the magnetic properties of lodestones were discovered long ago, ancient scientists pursued this path, which led to the control of energy by magnetic means.

An attempt to create a worldwide broadcast energy system caused a massive disruption to the Earth's magnetic field which brought on the equivalent of a nuclear winter.

The resulting global devastation brought civilization to its knees and those few small groups who retained vestiges of the old technology were looked upon as magicians—or Spellbinders.

Bruce Sterling: My imagination tends to be captured by especially colorful scenes and situations. It helps if they have some thematic relevance to current events. *Difference Engine*, for instance, is a book about the social impact of computation, written by a couple of cyberpunk guys who are genuinely troubled by the social impact of computation.

Michael Swanwick: Reading, cultivating a sense of the absurd, wishful thinking, daydreaming …

Harry Turtledove: I'm an SF writer with a doctorate in Byzantine history. I take science fictional extrapolation techniques and apply them to the past rather than the future. I read a lot. I think a lot—it's about all I'm good for, and being good at it, as you'll know yourself,

I daresay, helps a lot less than people who aren't so good at it commonly believe.

Janeen Webb: The ideas are always there—the "what if ... " scenarios are always with us. The problem is deciding which of the possibilities will turn out to be worth the huge amount of time and research it takes to put flesh on the narrative bones.

George Zebrowski: Alternate history ideas come to me out of the physics of "the sum over histories," out of the psychological sweetness of "what might have been" but wasn't, out of the inertia we see in human history, which changes so much outside and so little within—unless we become transhuman. But most of all I must see a non-trivial point to the story other than the novelty. Pamela Sargent did this in her novel *Climb the Wind*.

Can you give any examples of inspirations, revelations, or incidents that triggered the idea for a counterfactual novel or story?

Terry Bisson: I have written two Alt history novels. *In Fire On the Mountain*, Harriet Tubman takes part in John Brown's raid on Harper's Ferry (doesn't fall ill), the raid succeeds, and thus the Civil War is started by the abolitionists and the result is an independent black socialist nation in the South. In *Any Day Now*, Robert Kennedy and Martin Luther King both survive, and the USA dissolves into civil war; meanwhile a Bolshevik renaissance in The Soviet Union leads toward the collapse of US Imperialism worldwide. Thus three events!

Any Day Now was directly inspired by Roth's *The Plot Against America*, in which a charismatic Lindbergh "steals" the Republican nomination and defeats Roosevelt. I added the wounded Kennedy to Chicago '68.

John Crowley: I spent a long winter's afternoon once trying to think of a way I could make a lot of money from going into the past. Just once. I tried to make my fantasy as realistic as possible (all but the time-travel part.) My thoughts—and the solution I hit on—are in the chapter "The Single Excursion of Caspar Last" that opens *Great Work of Time*.

Paul Di Filippo: Believe it or not, the genesis of the project described above happened when I was walking through the campus of Brown University during the first week of an autumn semester.

The freshmen were having an "orientation" which consisted of playing Twister on the lawn. I started thinking what Thomas Wolfe (1900–38) would have made of such a scene when he in all mature seriousness arrived at Harvard.

Lisa Goldstein: When I was very young, maybe too young, I read a history of the Jews that my parents had lying around the house. I was horrified by the seemingly endless accounts of killings, executions, tortures, and pogroms, and I remember that the part about Muslim Spain seemed to come as an oasis, a break in an otherwise long and terrible history. Then, after 9/11, when anti-Arab feeling grew and people started to say outrageous or ridiculous things about Muslims, I remembered this book.

Then you asked me for a story, and I tried to do some research. I couldn't find what I wanted so I gave up on the idea—until years later, when someone recommended a book called *The Ornament of the World*. Turns out more histories had been written in the meantime, and I was able to plot out the story.

Part of the inspiration for the story was the anger I felt at the ignorant things people were saying, which is perhaps why this is the only alternate history I ever wrote. It was a lot of fun, though, and I'd definitely like to write another one.

Richard Harland: Okay, I've just given one. Here's another that bears on the world of juggernauts in *Worldshaker* and *Liberator*. The general socio-cultural principle is that small, isolated "colonies" tend to preserve the original culture much longer than the mother-society from which they came. For example, the Greek community in Melbourne; for example, the way the United States in the nineteenth century preserved older pronunciations and speech-forms long after they'd been displaced in Britain. (Cultural preservation in spite of/ because of other changes made necessary by a new and unfamiliar environment.) Similarly, society on board the juggernauts has remained stuck in the Victorian mold long after its natural use-by date has passed. Given the way the juggernauts have cut themselves off from external influences for over a hundred years, there has been nothing to alter their inhabitants' way of thinking—only a sentimental, identity-affirming attachment to the Old Country as it was when they left it.

Technology on board the juggernauts has stayed stuck in a steam-age rut too. However, I was aware of another historical principle in relation to construction of the juggernauts in the middle of the nineteenth century—as remarkable feats of engineering far beyond anything that could have been constructed at that time in real history. However, I had my alternate Fifty Years War preceding the juggernauts—and it's an established fact that the rate of technological advance typically speeds up during a war. With a whole fifty years of wartime competition, well, it seemed obvious that there would be a huge leap in industrialization over that period, along with a hyper-development of certain forms of technology.

Charlaine Harris: In Lizbeth's case, I wanted to write about a young woman who shoots a lot of people ... but she couldn't go to jail every time. The whole world arose from those two things.

John Kessel: My story of Bush and Castro as baseball players originated when I saw a note in Harper's magazine that talked about Fidel Castro being scouted for the NY Giants and the Pittsburgh Pirates as a pitcher in the late 1940s. When I read later that George H.W. Bush had also been a baseball player, I saw the opportunity for a political allegory.

My story "Buffalo," which is a very minor alternate history, came when I read in H. G. Wells's biography that he had been in Washington in 1934, at the same time my father was in the Civilian Conservation Corps in northern Virginia.

My story "The Invisible Empire" came from a paragraph in Karen Joy Fowler's story "Game Night at the Fox and Goose" where a character describes briefly an alternate history where women formed terrorist groups, a kind of feminist KKK, in the late 1800s to anonymously avenge outrages against women by men.

Kim Stanley Robinson: Once after reading John Hershey's *Hiroshima*, I had a vision of a B-29 bomber, headed toward Japan, tilting over and shooting straight down into the ocean. That inspired the story.

In the late 1970s, thinking specifically about alternative history, it occurred to me that if the Black Death had killed everyone in Europe then the history of the world would have gone very differently. This I had to hold onto for twenty years before I knew enough about novel writing to write the idea down.

I wrote "A Sensitive Dependence on Initial Conditions" because I wasn't comfortable with the long-term alternative history suggested at the end of "The Lucky Strike." I wanted to write more alternatives. This was a kind of meta-story, composed of second thoughts, five or seven years after the first story was written.

Mary Rosenblum: My Aboriginal America world was inspired by reading an account of Zheng He, the eunuch court mariner who explored to India and the American continent. If China had continued, I thought, if they had at least partially defeated small pox, what would the Europeans have found on the American continent? A small political change in China could have profoundly altered world history.

Pamela Sargent: My story "Hillary Orbits Venus" was triggered by the following true incident: the fifteen-year-old Hillary Rodham (later to become Hillary Rodham Clinton) wrote to NASA asking what she should do and study to become an astronaut. Somebody at NASA wrote back to tell her that no females need apply. I immediately thought: What if instead somebody had written back to encourage her? The whole story grew from there. I might add that in this story Bill Clinton still has a career as a politician and becomes president, as that seemed his likely fate in most continua.

Bruce Sterling: I like the design of period technology. It was great that difference engines didn't really exist, but were also such a striking material instantiation of high Victorian technology—big brass clockworks, a kind of high-performance super-lathe.

Michael Swanwick: 1. Thirty years ago, I got one chapter into a novel about time-traveling confidence artists before losing interest in it. I'd given a copy of that chapter to Gardner Dozois, however, and one day I dropped by his apartment to discover him busily typing. He ripped the sheet out of his typewriter, added it to a sheaf of papers and handed it to me, saying, "Congratulations, you've written an alternate history story!" And I had. He'd removed the first and last pages and written a new opening and conclusion, changing one of the characters into a member of the Time Police, charged with patrolling alternate timelines. It was just that easy.

2. "The Gods of Mars," written with Gardner Dozois and Jack Dann, is what might be called a Schrodinger's Cat Story—one with two possible explanations, one of which is an alternate history. It was inspired by a recurrent conversation that Gardner and I had over the fact, then well known, that a sandstorm blew up to cover

Mars just as the first probe was entering a position to send back photographs of its surface. "What if," one of us said, "the planet looked like Edgar Rice Burroughs' Mars before the sandstorm and our contemporary Mars after?"

3. My alternate history novel *Jack Faust* was inspired by reading Christopher Marlowe's *Doctor Faustus* at age sixteen and feeling strongly that the premise required Faustus to be damned by the knowledge he'd sold his soul for, rather than the mere fact of having sold his soul. When I finally decided to write the novel, as an adult, I employed Isaac Asimov's *The Gods Themselves* as the mannequin, and thus the jonbar point was Faust's conjuring up not demons but aliens from a much hotter parallel universe.

Harry Turtledove: Judy Tarr was complaining in a letter in 1988 that the cover art for a historical fantasy novel she had coming out was as anachronistic as Robert E. Lee with an Uzi. I looked at that and admired it. When I wrote back, I printed out the letter and added a handscrawl PS under my signature: "Who'd want to give Robert E. Lee an Uzi? Time-traveling South Africans, maybe? If I write it, I'll give you an acknowledgment." I liked that a lot, so I made sure to save a Xerox before I sent it off. And that's how *Guns of the South* happened, and how I got to quit my day job. Thanks, Judy …

Janeen Webb: In the case of *The Five Star Republic*, the trigger was a chance convention discussion on ecopunk and the future of solar energy. Panellists were asked "what if solar power had been pursued in the 1970s?"; we took it back another hundred years, and asked "what if solar power had been pursued in the 1870s?" It was perfectly possible—John Ericsson's Sun Engine was up and running then, as were many other solar powered steam engines. We extrapolated from there, to create a counterfactual history we wish we'd had—a vision of hope rather than a prophecy of doom.

George Zebrowski: Regarding a "jonbar hinge" (presumably referring to Jack Williamson's *The Legion of Time*). One of these for me was the story that German submarines patrolled off Dover during the Second World War in the hope of hitting Eisenhower with their artillery, since he was known to take a jeep ride there at times. I used this fact in one of my "history machine" stories, and was told by Paul Carter that this was a gratuitous use of history; but I informed him it was "real."

Nevertheless, it sounds gratuitous, like much of alternate history, but it got me thinking about selecting "pointed" examples beyond their aesthetic/dramatic value. Gliders at Thermopylae is pretty but pointless. Pointed choices of a hinge might be known by how painful they are—in my "Lenin in Odessa" Russian history comes out about the same for Stalin, which led one reviewer to note that he couldn't tell real history from mock.

Anything else come to mind?

Michael Bishop: I'll make a stab at answering your question about alternate-history sf. Right now I'm preparing to write, and should be writing, an introduction for a Polish edition of the first volume of the *Collected Stories of Philip K. Dick*, that volume being *The Short Happy Life of the Brown Oxford*. To write my intro, I had to order a used copy of that volume (because although I own nearly fifty of Dick's books, novels and previous story collections, I didn't have that one); and in this hefty trade paperback, when it arrived, I was delighted to find, a short but quite dense preface by Dick, excerpted from a letter that he wrote to someone (I don't know whom) on May 14, 1981, not quite ten months before his death. That it advocates passionately for the notion that all of SF represents a type of alternate-history seems a serendipitous thing, considering what you've asked me to comment on, and I hope you'll forgive me for conflating my assignment from Poland and your personal request.

In the epistolary excerpt, Dick gives his own definition of science fiction, which he calls "sf" (not "SF"), remarking that SF creates "a fictitious world; that is the first step: it is a society that does not in fact exist, but is predicated on our known society; that is, our known society acts as a jumping-off point for it; the society advances out of our own in some way, perhaps orthogonally, as with the alternate world story or novel. It is our world dislocated by some kind of mental effort on the part of the author, our world transformed into that which it is not or not yet."

Clearly, I'm stealing here, but I can't say it any better than Dick does, so forgive me for quoting further as Dick goes on to note, "[The] world must differ from the given in at least one way, and this way must be sufficient to give rise to events that could not occur in our society—or in any known society present or past. There must be a coherent idea involved in this dislocation; that is, the dislocation must be a conceptual one, not merely a trivial or bizarre one—this is the essence of science fiction, the conceptual dislocation within the society so that as a result a new society is generated in the author's mind, transferred to paper [or, presumably, a computer screen], and from the paper [or the digital file] it occurs as a convulsive shock in the reader's mind, the shock of dysrecognition." Dick also remarks that the reader understands that this society is not his or her "actual world," but nevertheless finds the dislocation within it fascinating, "intellectually stimulating" to the point that it "unlocks the reader's mind, so that that mind, like the author's, begins to create. Thus SF is creative, and it inspires creativity."

I rarely if ever write a novel or story on the basis of a coherent structuring thesis, and I don't think Dick did either. In fact, I believe that in the foregoing passages, Dick describes in thoughtful retrospect what his own SF does and how it accomplishes what it does, but that, while writing fiction, he worked intuitively to create the effects that they achieve. Still, Dick's definition resonates with me profoundly. In fact, when I saw the words dislocated and dislocation in his definition of sf, I had a shock of recognition (not of dysrecognition, a characteristic coinage of Dick's). In May of 2013, you see, I was the only featured American writer of SF at Italcon 39, held in the lovely coastal town of Bellaria, and to honor that fact, the man who invited me, Armando Corridore, owner of the Bologna-based publishing firm Elara, translated my alternate-history novelette "The Quickening" into Italian and offered it at the convention as a small stand-alone entitled *Dislocazione*. Indeed, a buyer of any other *Elara* title at all received it as a lagniappe.

Apparently, the word quickening, meaning the kinetic development of an embryo in a woman's womb (or, I assume, that of any mammal), has no exact counterpart in Italian, and so, perceptively, Armando settled on *dislocazione* as an appropriate substitute for the English-language title for my story. In any case, "The Quickening" concerns what I view as an extremely nontrivial alteration in human society, namely, the mysterious overnight redistribution of every human being on our planet to another part of the globe. This is not an idea that many people would regard as science-based; in fact, most would define it as fantastic if not as utterly ludicrous, but I developed it with total seriousness, and in its year of eligibility, the story won a Nebula Award for best novelette. All of the preceding, then, clearly shows that in my own writing of alternate history, I intuitively follow the intuitive practice of Philip K. Dick, although I have his work as a guide, and Dick developed his techniques and approaches largely on his own (for none of us are without influences).

Other works of mine that employ Dick's approaches and techniques—again, more or less intuitively, albeit in one noteworthy case with a methodical consciousness—include the novels *Unicorn Mountain, Count Geiger's Blues*, and, of course, *Philip K. Dick Is Dead, Alas* (a.k.a. *The Secret Ascension*). The primary dislocation in the last-named novel focuses on the horrifically extended presidency of a diabolically possessed Richard Nixon, a US victory in the war in Vietnam, and the establishment of a base on the Moon during my Nixon's long tenancy in the Oval Office. Philip K. Dick is of course a character in these proceedings, but the novel focuses on the actions and interactions of "little people," people without world-shaking authority, just as the real Philip K. Dick's novels and stories consistently, almost obsessively, do.

Incidentally, I did not originally admire Dick for his style, thinking it workmanlike and journalistic, but it improved (at least in my view) as his career progressed; and when Ursula K. Le Guin (my favorite SF writer in the late 1960s) released *The Lathe of Heaven* (1971), a deliberate take on Dick's techniques and thematic preoccupations, she validated for me what he was up to, and I went back to his Hugo Award-winning *The Man in the High Castle* and read him with more sympathy and more understanding. My comic story "Rogue Tomato," which sold to Robert Silverberg's *New Dimensions 5* (1975), even features a protagonist, Philip K., who represents an outrageous forerunner of the dislocated characters in "The Quickening," so that the story itself functions, perhaps, as a warm-up for the writing of *Philip K. Dick Is Dead, Alas*.

Paul Di Filippo: Steampunk seems to have colonized and dominated the alternate history genre of late, narrowing the medium's infinite possibilities. That seems wrong-headed and unfortunate to me.

Charlaine Harris: My world building starts with a kernel and then grows. It's always based on the character I'm writing about.

Christopher Priest: Moving on to the third part [of your questionnaire], I'd rather give you a general answer than try to reply to the specific queries. This is because I'm likely to go on giving you negative specific answers, which won't get you or me anywhere, whereas in general I feel interested in the subject and want to support what you are doing.

As I'm principally a novelist like you, and not a theorist like Shippey, I can really only see this subject through my own work. I hope this bit won't bore you.

My last three novels are virtually unknown outside the UK and Europe, so I suspect you haven't had a chance to read them. *The Separation* could not find a trade edition in the United States, and ended up in an expensive small-press hardback. *The Islanders* could not find an American publisher at all. My most recent novel, *The Adjacent*, will be published next year in the United States, but by Titan, who are based in the UK. Titan will be publishing *The Islanders* at the same time, in paperback. All three are in some senses counterfactual, although only *The Separation* comes close to the sort of novel you are interested in. The other two are "psychological" counterfactuals, dealing with, if you like, alternative ways of understanding the past, present and future. In *The Adjacent*, this process is made more explicit than in the other two ... so in that sense the three should be read together. The book I'm working on at the moment continues this examination of reality.

I hope I'm not losing you.

The Separation posits one of the counterfactual ideas you mention: a different outcome to the Second World War. In broad brush-strokes: a separate peace between Britain and Germany was briefly possible in the early months of 1941. I assumed that the Churchill government negotiated with the Nazis (highly improbable in the real world) and established an armistice. The consequences of this are suggested but not described in detail.

But there is no single divergent point. There is a series of events, roughly covering six months, which might or might not be relevant: the story is told through the lives of two brothers, identical twins, who themselves have diverged (or separated—the title). One is a conscientious objector who tries to work for peace, the other is in the RAF, employed in destroying German cities. At different points in the novel both brothers are killed, or are believed to be killed.

They are constantly muddled up by the authorities, including by Churchill, who meets them both at different times. Then there is a young Jewish refugee who meets both brothers, comes to Britain, marries one of them, has an affair with the other, and bears a child ... the identity (and parentage and even gender) of the child is never certain. And finally, there is the question of Rudolf Hess, who flew to Scotland in 1941 with a peace plan, apparently authorized by Hitler. Hess also meets both brothers at different times, with widely differing consequences.

I saw *The Separation* as being specifically about the process of historical change. The Hess affair alone is full of many unanswered questions (including, as a matter of interest, a long-standing theory that it was not Hess at all—the theory of a Hess double has been attacked and "disproved" several times, but the questions remain unanswered). The Hess affair also suggests several different ways of interpreting events that followed. Hess, for instance, had no idea that Japan and the USA would join the war, although historically this seems inevitable now.

Anyway, the point really is that *The Separation* both is and is not the sort of counterfactual novel you're interested in, and directly answers most of your questions in part three. I hope this is a satisfactory response, and doesn't seem too self-serving.

Kim Stanley Robinson: You should write a sequel to *The Rebel* and *Promised Land*, as I suggested in the introduction to the latter, because you have left us hanging with RFK still about to become president in 1968 (if I recall right), and therefore what you were suggesting about history itself is obscured or left hanging fire. However, it would present a big problem to you, or so it seems to me; could RFK have changed anything? If so, what? Etc. A wicked challenge that could be super interesting.

Also, I would make a distinction between "counter-factuals," which are historian's exercises to illustrate a point, thin texture, essay format, weak or useless, poorly regarded in historian's arguments, a rhetorical device (probably named in Greek as such!) and "Alternative history," which is a sub-genre of science fiction, with thick texture that makes it powerfully persuasive, including some great novels that make worlds of their own, great historical commentaries; essentially, *better* than counter-factuals as a genre.

Pamela Sargent: I might have pushed the boundaries a bit in my novel *Climb the Wind*, which was inspired by a comment Louis L'Amour (one of my father's favorite writers, as he was a fan of Westerns) made during an interview: "The history of the United States would have been very different if there had been an Indian Genghis Khan." A number of my characters, both real historical figures and invented characters, have visions, as some of them (Crazy Horse) did in real life. (Visions were an important part of Plains Indian culture.) In these visions, some of them see what happened to them or those near them in our world, as opposed to their world. That might seem to make this novel more of a magic realist or historical fantasy work than alternate history. But something was telling me that leaving out any role for visions wouldn't be true to some of the cultures I was depicting, and the visions also served as a commentary on alternative time lines.

Originally I saw *Climb the Wind* as a companion to my historical novel *Ruler of the Sky*, which had Genghis Khan as its central character. I thought it would end with an Indian conquest of the eastern US, but their victory turned out to be a lot more ambiguous. To have had the kind of triumphant ending I had originally expected would have been sheer wish fulfillment and, given historical inertia, implausible.

Lewis Shiner: Most of my story ideas start with a tingle, kind of like Spider-Man's "spidey sense." To start with one specific example, I had been reading for years about Nikola Tesla and, in parallel, about the Columbian Exhibition in Chicago in 1893. Both those subjects gave me that tingle. When my sense of a possible story reached a certain critical mass, I started reading Margaret Cheney's *Tesla: Man Out of Time*. Cheney at one point starts listing all the ideas Tesla had recorded in his notebooks that he never got around to completing, and one of them was the "Terrestrial Night Light," a plan to electrically charge the ionosphere so that the earth would be illuminated twenty-four hours a day.

My brain responded like a pinball machine when you've hit the jackpot, with all kinds of buzzers and lights. This was the best example I'd ever heard of science trampling over sentiment simply because it could. It also dovetailed with many of Tesla's personal quirks, and made me understand that, unlike the weirdo hero many people thought Tesla to be, he was, for me, a monster.

The "White City" of the Columbian Exposition seemed to be a similar sort of thing: Art and culture and food and technology from around the world being plundered in the name of modernity and science. What better place for Tesla to carry out his fiendish plan?

In a sense, the resulting story, also called "White City," is alternate history—obviously Tesla did not create this experiment in our world. I was not concerned, however, with the point at which our histories diverged—I didn't care why Tesla never completed the experiment, or what would have had to change in history to get him to that point. For me the story functions more as reductio ad absurdum—this is where science, without compassion, leads.

The closest I've come to a "typical" alternate history story is probably "The Death of Che Guevara." The initial impulse came from a conversation with a friend in Buenos Aires, where Che is still revered as a hero and where you can buy postcards featuring images of him on every street corner, along with those of the tango singer Carlos Gardel and the saintly Eva Perón. I was expressing my concern about idealizing a revolutionary who carried (and used) a gun, and my friend, the Argentine writer Sergio Gaut vel Hartman, said that the thing that bothered him the most was Che's executions—the thousands of people he had ordered put to death. On the other hand, I had heard speeches by Che that moved me deeply, and I admired a lot of his ideals. I knew I wanted to write something about my mixed feelings, and as I began my research (mostly using Jon Lee Anderson's excellent *Che*) it quickly became clear that to get to the bottom of this enigma, Che would have to live longer.

Now, in this case it just happened that there was exactly the sort of pivotal moment that Tom Shippey talks about: Shortly before Che's death in Bolivia, he had to split his forces. On their way to rejoin Che, the second contingent was betrayed and slaughtered. One miniscule change could have saved them and possibly prevented Che's death, with, indeed, massive consequences. Again, however, I was not so much interested in the change for its own sake, but rather to make a political point, to again do a sort of reductio ad absurdum where Che could reveal himself to be less a dedicated lifelong revolutionary than a contrarian, a trickster, and a deeply conflicted human being. To put it another way, I was not doing an experiment to see what might happen if I pushed this domino over rather than that, but rather to bend history so I could make a point.

You can see this impulse at work in a few of my other stories. In "Twilight Time" a time-traveling character deliberately exploits what we might call a "Shippey Point" to try to change the future. In "Primes" two parallel worlds, which diverged at a Shippey Point where Clinton was caught with his pants down right before the 1992 election, are conflated and the two are examined side by side. I think there's some metafictional stuff going on there, where in both cases the process of extrapolation is laid bare. That's even more true in my novel *Glimpses* where the protagonist again is trying to exploit (or even create) Shippey points to change music history. In the short stories, there is again a political impulse at work. Both alternate societies are conservative and repressive, both reductios of trends that were current at the time. And while there isn't much politics in *Glimpses*, in this case the hero's life is reduced to a sort of caricature to make a point about his psychological state.

I should probably at least mention my most-reprinted alternate history story, "Mozart in Mirrorshades." The setup came entirely from Bruce,[3] and he was very explicit about the point he wanted to make: time travelers exploiting the past as an allegory for the exploitation of the third world. I drafted the first half of the story, and so did a lot of the extrapolation—but this doesn't fall under Shippey's definition. To have time travelers show up and start pumping oil out of your ground is not minor, especially if they are at the same time bringing drugs, sex, and rock and roll to the locals.

To recap, alternate history, for me, is usually a tool to create an exaggerated or distilled version of the present—a way to set up an environment that I can then manipulate to make a particular point.

Bruce Sterling: I once wrote an alternate history story, "Dori Bangs," which was just about some historical guy accidentally meeting some historical woman he never actually met. This story disobeys practically all your concepts; the lead figures care nothing for history, history is not all changed by their liaison, they make no big difference from their small novum, and the story is not about history per se, it's basically about mortality, and about personal life decisions, such as, "Am I really going to marry this lunatic although I should know better?" It's one of my most popular stories. People find it moving in a way that most Jonbar changes fail to convey.

---

[3]Bruce Sterling.

Michael Swanwick: The alternate history is probably the easiest form of science fiction there is to write shoddily, and no harder to write well than any other sub-form of the genre.

Howard Waldrop: One of the tragedies of the field is that alt. hist. has become just another sub-genre of SF. As somebody said, "Once, *all* alt. hist. stories were swell and memorable; now there are so many lots are *not.*"

I'll still try to keep writing about better and brighter pasts, when the idea for one comes up.

Janeen Webb: Alternate history and counterfactual history are discussed together here, but I do think there is a substantive difference, in that alternate history allows the inclusion of historically impossible elements (such as the introduction of modern weaponry into the timeframe of the American Civil War in Harry Turtledove's *Guns of the South*), whereas counterfactual history does not.

Any general or specific ideas concerning the craft of writing alternate history?

Terry Bisson: The craft of writing is about the same for everything. I think Alt. History, like hard SF, has to be a bit stricter than most SF. And like most SF, it's not really the place for experimental prose styles. The more ordinary the better.

In most alt histories the divergence point is seen as a flashback from the alt world. This is I think the easier way. In *Any Day Now* I led up to it gradually, with little less important changes. Which most people never even noticed! So as in any fiction you have to think hard about where to begin your story.

William Gibson: My favorite authors of alternate history have been Amis, Dick, Nabokov and Keith Roberts. And each on the basis, remarkably, of a single novel. I think that that indicates that it's a very difficult thing to do really well.

Lisa Goldstein: I write a lot of historical fantasy and just finished a time-travel novel, and I have to say I enjoy research, learning about different times and cultures, finding out that things were a lot more complicated than what's generally known, or even completely the opposite of what most people think. I like immersing myself in a culture, figuring out how people lived then. Also, while you're doing research you can tell yourself you're actually working, even if all you're doing is reading. This is probably an impetus for why I wrote an alternate history.

Charlaine Harris: Don't spend so much time constructing the world that you neglect to write the book.

Barry N. Malzberg: I will try to help you but the academic jargon and the queries themselves give me the vapors. I do not mind discussing my work at all but to do so in terms acceptable to PMLA imposes nausea. What I can try is a short, informal essay on the subject.

I gave these stories next to no (prior) thought but wrote them and learned by going where I had to go. "In the Stone House," among the best of them (many of these are Kennedy-centered of course) is based upon a plot Mike Resnick gave me. (It appeared in his anthology *Alternate Kennedys*.) "Fugato" (Leonard Bernstein gets drafted and dies in the Battle of the Bulge), is a notional story based upon the profound effect his performance of the *Symphonie Fantastique* on 6/2/62 with the Philharmonic (the last concert the Philharmonic ever gave at Carnegie, moving in September to the space at Lincoln Center) had on me as direct witness. There are a lesser flock of such notional stories (Toscanini Americanized as "Art Tosca" is the manager of Babe Ruth and the 1927 Yankees), Lee Harvey Oswald is JFK's Appointments Secretary), not all of which are embarrassing. My own favorite among them is "Heavy Metal" (*Alternate Presidents* edited by Mike Resnick) in which JFK loses the 1960 Presidential election. As author of *The Rebel* you know as much or more about this genre than anyone alive and you know what a mug's game it is, Roth's *The Plot Against America* being a gorgeous example of its futility. (Roth, our greatest writer, runs his premise and its carload right off the rails.) The Alternate History or Counterfactual Story achieved great currency in the 1980s (it was a marginal form in the 1950s), science fiction marking for me the plunge of our field into decadence, into the eating (world-snake fashion) of its own tail.

Kim Stanley Robinson: It's good to remember that around or outside the changed events of the story, the stuff that stays the same will stay the same, and still be interesting, even for contrast. In *Years*, I had the Europeans die out in 1420 or so, but that still meant that Akbar was the same in India much later, and even

China in 1776 was not demonstrably different from the China in our world in 1776, because European contacts with east Asia were trivial until 1800 or 1830. This in itself is interesting, when contemplating world history.

Mary Rosenblum: I work with a *lot* of novice and aspiring authors and the biggest issue I see is the focus on plot with the alternate history world details pasted in as window dressing. That is, in my opinion, totally the wrong way to come at this, resulting in a story that has no real need to be set anywhere but in the present.

Pamela Sargent: See my essay "Science Fiction, Historical Fiction, and Alternative History," in *The Bulletin of the Science Fiction and Fantasy Writers of America* 29 (Fall, 1995).

Bruce Sterling: Reading old histories is a good idea. Then you can see that history is quite mutable, it's a kind of retrodiction. There are so many different versions of, say, the career of Napoleon that they're practically counterfactual narratives as they stand.

Lately I've been writing and lecturing rather a lot about a concept called "atemporality." I lack the time to explain it here, but conceivably it might help you.

Here are some pictures that try to suggest what I mean. http://www.flickr.com/photos/brucesterling/sets/72157619722832388/

Michael Swanwick: Samuel R. Delany once wrote that "Everything in a science fiction novel should be mentioned at least twice (in at least two different contexts)." Two clear statements of whatever it is that makes the alternate history different from our own seem to be not only sufficient but a maximum. More than that and the reader will feel hectored.

Harry Turtledove: See my "Alternate History: the How-to of What Might Have Been," in Michael Knost, ed., *Writers Workshop of Science Fiction and Fantasy* (Seventh Star Press, no place of publication shown, 2013).

Howard Waldrop: You have to decide how much alike the world is, i.e. McDonald's but no Ace Hardwares, etc. What cars are on the roads, which aren't, etc.

The hinge points can be as small or as large as the concerns of the story dictate. In "The World, as We Know't" the concerns are large—the phlogiston theory is the *real* physics there, and things follow accordingly. This fits the Shippey definition of "massive in consequence." Others, like in "The Lions Are Asleep This Night" the deep idea is that there *were* no inhabitants of the New World when found by Europeans. But this is buried in a story about a kid in a revivified Africa writing an Elizabethan Revenge Play, which reflects on the cultural facts of *his* time and place. This is small in itself (it barely figures in the story) except that the revivified Africa is a result of a past slave revolt (in the New World) since slaves would have to be imported in greater numbers to take the place of non-existent Amerindians to the Europeans of the story.

George Zebrowski: As someone who is well aware of the various "philosophies" of history, meaning answers to the question "what are we to make out of history?" and "how reliable is historical data?" Better still, "what is the truth content in historical writings, both of past times and in the present?," which make me turn at once to a book entitled *The Uses of the Past*, which undermines the credibility of so-called historical data, but not entirely; it turns us instead to the explanatory function of storytelling. Everything we think and write is a story, everything is history; time underlies everything in a baffling way. Historical thought itself has a history to be examined.

As one philosopher has said, if historical accounts don't show some relevance to our present, or future, human condition, then they are of antiquarian interests only (like Civil War reenactments) and should be consigned to the lumber room of history.

This has led me to think that alternate histories in SF come with a face value of triviality, arbitrariness, odd curiosity, and such— unless there is some clear pointedness to a scenario which joins it to some irony, mockery, even to an anarchic bitterness about the present or a possible future. This makes most alternate histories mere extravagances, gratuitous—

But all of them can be justified by the physics of "the sum over histories" which claims that *all* imaginable histories are real, if unreachable, however silly (there's one in which I wear only black shoelaces, for example), but do any of us truly wish to write about them? Fredric Brown's *What Mad Universe* does so, but how often can this trick be performed? See also my *Stranger Suns* for a shuffling of histories.

So, I end up with "pointedness" as an impulsive reason for writing an alternate history—but I fear a mill-like industry which wears out its welcome. My story, "Lenin in Odessa" received the comment that the critic couldn't tell the real history from what happened—which was one of my underlying points of psychology, as in *Stranger Suns*. "Lenin in Odessa" might even be true, as a guess of what happened to the spy Sidney Reilly and to Lenin.

My bottom line about alternate histories is that I would write them infrequently, sparingly, when some pointedness nags at you with its irony and moral stance, not with simple cleverness. Of course, with commerce, if a little bit is good, then the whole bottle is better, and the mouse must enchant the brooms to carry endless buckets of water until the sorcerer takes pity on him and stops the show.

Fiction is a multi-ring circus, and anything that can be written will be written, and the past will speak to us through our eyeglasses of concern and fear, and great is the writer who can discern these fears and byways and glimpse through their thickets some signs of what is truly happening to us in the unfoldings of time.

Why do you write this stuff and ... ?

Andrew Enstice: Well, apart from the (considerable) pleasures of research and collaboration, allowing the space to imagine a world other than the one we now inhabit offers something of a relief valve. We may be largely powerless in the realms of politics and high finance, but in the reader's head we can—possibly—divert the course of the Titanic just enough to suggest the possibility of avoiding the fatal collision. And who knows, if just one of those readers is in a better position to take the real helm ...

Terry Bisson: My work in Alt. History is inspired by my socialist and utopian leanings. I strive to make it as realistic as possible.

Paul Di Filippo: I treat my alternate history stories as just another subgenre, no more nor less interesting than the other tropes of SF. One day I might want to write about "first contact" with aliens, while another day I might want to write about a timeline where geeks rule the Earth ("Murder in Geektopia").

Charlaine Harris: Keeps me off the streets.

John Kessel: To me the power of alternate history is its essential irony—the distance between what we know really happened and what we presume to have happened in our invented alternative world. It only works if you know the real history, and have some sort of opinion about it, or it has some emotional resonance for you.

Kim Stanley Robinson: I like history, and science fiction is a historical form of fiction, it contains its future history that connects back to now.

My definition of science fiction is that it is "the history we can never know," which has three branches: the future; alternative histories; and pre-history, the human time before written history gave us those stories. This is why all three of these sub-genres are all in the science fiction part of the bookstores and done by the same writers often. They are all three "historical" in nature, but concern histories that will always remain unavailable to us, but interesting anyway. I first put forth this theory in an article about Cecelia Holland published in *Foundation* in 1986 or 1987. "Some Notes Toward an Essay on Cecelia Holland," I think it was called. This might help you to situate alternative history in science fiction and among the other sub-genres.

Mary Rosenblum: It is fascinating to think about alternatives, should events have played out differently. Personally, I think our ability to ask "what if" is the foundation of our humanity. It is what makes us human. So hey, why not?

Pamela Sargent: At least partly because historical fiction was some of my favorite reading as a child, and alternate history allows me to explore in fictional form "what might have been" (as opposed to science fiction, which is more about "what could be." Because sometimes I just want to escape the here and now. Because I was always aware of how chancy my own existence was: if my father had died in combat during the Second World War, I would never have been born. If he had stayed in California after the war and gone into show business (as he had wanted to do, in radio, movies and early TV) instead of coming back East under pressure from his father, after my mother got pregnant with me, to finish his education and pursue a more practical occupation, my family's life would have been entirely different. I used to play imaginatively with these alternative lives as a kid. I suppose that, like all children, I was the Jonbar hinge that altered my parents' lives.

Mark Shirrefs: Because it's fun to play God.

Bruce Sterling: It's hard to say what's so attractive about the counterfactual, but I think it has something to do with issues of regret. It seems to come from wistful feelings of "I wish it hadn't been so." I don't think I've ever read a work of counter-historical fiction that is set in a placid period in which the protagonists cause awful, unnecessary havoc. Commonly they're about troubled times in which the author has some kind of solution to offer. I can't think of one about a nice time when the author creates unnecessary hell.

Michael Swanwick: The money.

Harry Turtledove: As noted before, I'm an SF writer with a history degree. A-h isn't all I write, not by a long chalk, but I do tend to think in such terms. And writing beats hell out of working for a living, which I've also done.

Howard Waldrop: People often ask me why I write alternate history, since most people don't even *know* the real history it diverges *from.* (I've had a panel on this at Readercon in Boston this year: how much *real* history must you refer to and not come off like a pedant?)

I usually say, "There's got to be a better (or differently interesting) one than *this* one, for God's sake. (The world we *have* was thought up by a Republican hack writer.)"

Janeen Webb: Like all writers, a large part of the answer to this question comes back to the sheer pleasure of creating something new in the world. As an academic, the realization that I can use the same research skills in a fictional context is liberating—I'd much rather be peer reviewed by counterfactual history readers than by an academic journal committee. A great deal of what looks like fiction in *The Five Star Republic* really did happen—it just got written out of history text books, so putting it back in fictional form, where it can reach a wider audience, feels totally appropriate.

George Zebrowski: I write few alternate histories, based on the [above] fear of pointless work, trivial concerns, and gratuitous juxtapositions. "A Hawk Among the Sparrows" by Dean McLaughlin pits a modern jet fighter against primitive aircraft with some great ironies: the wash from the jet runs the older craft, but the pilot of today has trouble distilling enough jet fuel to get himself in the air. Larger ironies about technology give the story more than its entertaining trivialities. Ward Moore's *Bring the Jubilee* gets far beyond its novelty.

Whatever I write, variant histories included, I do so for the act of shaping the work, for the beauty brought to me when I beat my own inability to produce the work. Oscar Wilde put it best in his baffling way (to blind readers) when he said that a man who makes a useful thing can be forgiven, as long as he does not admire what he has made, while the only excuse for making a useless thing is that one admires it intensely. Why so? Because such a work exists for itself, is not to be reduced to something else, or become a function of something else. He was speaking up for the absolute integrity of a beautiful work. Useful things abound, and do not have beauty's rare independence of slavery. A slave can possess beauty, as do money making works of fiction; they can even have artfulness—but not art. Consider the horror of great paintings which sell for millions, for money which might only have enabled the artist to paint more.

But the largest context of considerations in writing variant history stories, or even most science fiction, comes from the fact that all written histories are alternates, as our inquiries change over time. North and South American history is being vastly changed by forensic historiography, by forensic archeology (in which we see more than the two human types we thought we knew). Where we came from, who we are, and where are we going are still the great questions, deepening their insistence. Tentative history is all we have, and in science fiction we can rehearse as many as we can imagine.

What works for you?

Richard Harland: I've been jumping around all over the place—I think I've already given all my general and incidental comments!

Charlaine Harris: I'm still figuring that out!

Kim Stanley Robinson: I'm all done with alternative history, so this is a past tense question for me. What worked was reading a lot of histories with great pleasure, and then making the idea of the alternative take center stage. I think that's important, that alternative history can never be "just a backdrop."

Also, I would say that no matter what you do, alternative histories are rhetorically weak, compared to science fiction set in the future. Future SF says (like the ancient prophets): *This is going to happen.* It's very powerful in that sense. It warns, it beckons, it is an imperative, it commands attention. Alternative history, on the other hand, says: *This didn't happen, but if it had, it would have been interesting.* Well, so what? It doesn't establish or much support any theory of history, as being fictional and unconfirmable. It's almost like telling people your dream.

So, it needs to be compelling in ways that have nothing to do with theories of history, because it will never prove any case or persuade anyone of anything. At best, it can open up our feeling that history is something we make, and can still change in the present. That's its use value. It has a secondary value of making a new human world as a story space; without being fantastical, it still creates a new story space. That has a certain value. But it is not strong rhetorically, as any kind of argument.

Mary Rosenblum: What I most love in alt history is the change that alters not only historical events but the social fabric of the time, so that we see how mores, world view, religious focus, are intertwined with outside events to create history.

Pamela Sargent: Back in the early 1990s, I gave a talk at one convention in which I said that I had the persistent impression that all of us were living in a weird variant that had branched off from the main continuum, the main one being the timeline where we had settlements on Mars and more equitable social arrangements—in other words, the continuum where we were still looking hopefully toward the future. That feeling has persisted since then, and I have often wondered whether an interest in alternative history has grown out of a loss of hope, maybe even despair about a future that seems ever more problematic and threatening. The main continuum that I hypothesized in my speech and imaginings is one where the old folks (people my age) envy the young and the fascinating, hopeful universe they will inherit. I don't know too many old people who envy the young these days.

Mark Shirrefs: My best measure of what works is to ask the questions—is it fun? Which really means, does it inspire the imagination?

Bruce Sterling: History works for me. The metaphysics of the writing of history are interesting. How do we know how to write what we knew? How can we use language to make the past comprehensible to the future, when the past doesn't speak our language, and the future doesn't either?

Michael Swanwick: A well-told story that says something worth hearing. Also, the money.

Harry Turtledove: Story is easy. Style is at least moderately easy, unless I'm trying some special effect. Characters are hard for me; I'm not much of a people person, which is a drawback for a writer. So I work more on them.

Howard Waldrop: I try to do whatever the story needs to tell itself most effectively. (I'm often *wrong*.) That's just what stories *should* do, and alt. hist. is no different in that respect. Otherwise you end up with what Michael Bishop refers to as the "Duck, Mr. Lincoln" school of writing. Good alternate history stories should be more like Oscar Lewis' "The Lost Years" than *not*.

Janeen Webb: *The Five Star Republic* is a collaboration. The authors both have academic backgrounds as literary historians as well as writers, so we take advantage of our research experience to split the work between us (we are based in Australia, but there have been times when Andrew was in the UK and Janeen in the US, so it's vital that we are on the same page when it comes to digging through various archives). Our partnership is also successful in writing counterfactual history because we are able to combine different skill sets: Andrew's background as a screenwriter and dramatist, and Janeen's as a novelist and short story writer. The idea is that the finished product should be greater than the sum of its parts—a better book than either of us would have created alone—and that's the thing that works best for us.

George Zebrowski: I particularly like "small" divergences which loom large before the story is over. "A Sound of Thunder" by Bradbury, "The Brooklyn Project" by William Tenn, and especially "He Walked Around the Horses" by H. Beam Piper, where we are reminded of who Wellington was, to the bafflement of the narrator, and I suspect the puzzlement of many of today's readers.

#

So there you have it—many voices discussing the ins and outs and the hows and whys of counterfactual fiction. A diverse set of authors. A diverse set of ideas and approaches. In a sense, you've just passed through a maze of ideas, theories, and the many ways you might approach your own counterfactual fiction. Some of the writers' approaches to craft and story might feel antithetical to how you think and work. My hope—or, rather, expectation—is that some of these authors' ideas and craft workarounds will reinforce your own ideas, illuminate possibilities you hadn't thought of, and extend your range.

Pick and choose ... because in this particular instance you can't go wrong!

You might want to catch your breath before we take a deeper, more personal dive into the four central concepts that formed the basis of this Q & A chapter. There was a lot to take in.

##

7

A Very Personal Meditation on Writing

Or How I Do It ... and Think about It

I might mention that this personal meditation on my latest counterfactual novel and how I approach fiction in general is underpinned by the four concepts discussed in depth in the preceding chapter. This chapter is, in a sense, a working application of those concepts. I suggest you keep them in mind as you read ...

I am also aware that you might question why I'm using one of my own works as the basis of this chapter. If I intended this chapter to be a critical essay on counterfactual fiction, I would have referred to other writers and to second-hand experience; but this is not a critical essay. It is an attempt to give you an insight into the very process of conceiving and writing fiction ... it is an example of how this particular writer employs life experience, interests, and craft workarounds to produce a work of counterfactual fiction. And as I said in the previous chapter: if it speaks to you, if it reflects in some way how you work or might try working, that's great. If it is antithetical to your thinking processes, if it seems to be in opposition to your writing practice, that's fine, too. You might, however, find that the underlying ideas and descriptions of practice just might inform your own work.

#

It has been my experience as a writer that the initial "seed"—that numinous defining idea or inspiration, if you like—for short fiction and novels is either primarily visual or narrational.

Let me unpack my use of "narrational" as a descriptor for narration/plot. It is a term that has a particular resonance for me as a writer.

In his book *The Origin of Consciousness in the Breakdown of the Bicameral Mind,* Julian Jaynes employed the idea of narratization, of "seeing" through introspection, seeing "Things which you have never experienced except in this introspection" (34). For me, such "seeing" often takes the form of fictional "shapes" and plots, which often surface unbidden.

Jaynes writes that

> ... you can also rearrange your imaginal retrospection such that you do indeed 'see' entering the room just as it might have been; and 'hear' the sound of the chair and the book opening, and 'feel' the skin sensations. But I suggest that this has a large element of created imagery—what we shall call narratizing a little later—of what the experience should be like, rather than what it actually was like.
>
> (29)

And this idea of imaginal retrospection, in turn, resonates with my training in "the method" as an actor, which has profoundly influenced the way I write fiction.

The Silent, my historical novel about the American Civil War, came to me primarily as ... narratization. The catalyst was Jerzy Kosinski's introduction to his novel *The Painted Bird,* and in my afterword to *The Silent* I wrote:

> In Kosinski's introduction to a new edition of the book, he wrote that old school friends "blamed me for watering down historical truth and accused me of pandering to an Anglo-Saxon sensibility whose only confrontation with national cataclysm had been the Civil War a century earlier, when bands of abandoned children roamed through the devastated South." When I read that sentence, I was electrified. It was the shock of recognition. I knew, as soon as I read Kosinski's words, that my next major work would be about the Civil War ...
>
> As soon as I read Kosinski's lines, I glimpsed the thoughts and dreams and fears and obsessions of my protagonist: a

fourteen-year-old boy, mute from the horrors he has witnessed, chased by demons real and imagined, seeing the tragedy of the Civil War through a child's eyes where reality, folk superstition, magic, and history have become incandescent. I set out to portray the personal and secret world that exists within familiar textbook and popular history.

When I read Kosinski's comparison of *The Painted Bird* with the experience of children during the Civil War, I remembered how I had felt when I read *Lord of the Flies*, and I compared that experience to reading Kosinski's own *The Painted Bird*, Twain's *The Adventures of Huckleberry Finn*, and Salinger's *The Catcher in the Rye*. I could hear Mundy's voice whispering to me; and in that instant of "recognition" (for want of a better word), I knew how *The Silent* had to be shaped. The story required a close focus immediacy, and it had to be told from the most personal of viewpoints: first person ("A Note" 284).

The above is all true; but I left something out of that afterword: when I read those lines, when I was experiencing that dizzying moment of shall we say conceptualization, I saw the plot of the novel as if it were railroad tracks winding away ahead of me. I didn't know details and discovered many if not most of the plot intricacies as I progressed through the novel; but I "saw"[1] the novel as shape, as narrational plot arc—the obverse of how I saw/conceived my related renaissance novels *The Memory Cathedral* and *Shadows in the Stone*:

> *The Memory Cathedral* began in the lobby of the Algonquin Hotel in New York City. I was relaxing and enjoying reading Antonina Vallentin's 1938 biography of Leonardo Da Vinci when I suddenly saw in my mind's eye a squadron of high-gothic looking airplanes flying over Renaissance Florence; in fact, I saw the scene as if it were taking place in Giorgio Vasari's painting of Florence. I saw the planes passing over the Duomo, saw them reflected in the mirror of the Arno River that wound its way through Florence in Vasari's painting; and I knew, I knew then that I had to bring that image to life.
>
> But the image, when put to paper, was so transformed that I would hardly have recognized it.

---

[1]Narration has a synesthetic visual character for me; hence the conscious use of "saw."

Nevertheless, that's how it began; and I knew that if I was to bring this image to light and make it real, I would have to know my subject in such depth that what I put down on paper would only be the smallest part, the tip of the iceberg ("The Memory Cathedral" 10).

And like *The Memory Cathedral*, *Shadows in the Stone* came to me initially as image; not one overwhelming catalyzing image, but a series of images. The first and strongest images that come to mind just now as I reconstruct the creation of the novel are two illustrations depicting scenes from Milton's *Paradise Lost* (1667) by John Martin (1789–1834), an artist famous in his own time, but now largely forgotten (Turner 186). Two mezzotints, entitled "Pandemonium" (see Figure 1) and "Satan Presiding at the Infernal Council" (see Figure 2) seemed to me to encapsulate (or perhaps generated) my vision of the aeon Belias as dark angel and place.

In *Shadows* aeons, or higher angels, are depicted coextensively as beings and places. Thus the aeon Belias is both the presiding figure and the chiaroscuro defined landscape depicted in Martin's illustrations.

I had these images in mind when I wrote the following depiction of Pico Della Mirandola's young apprentice Pietro Neroni and the aeon Athoth journeying across Belias' empty, crystalline wastes as the theurgist Pico Della Mirandola falls into eternity, into the abyss of souls:

> In a sense Pietro and Athoth were stepping over or passing through the dark aeon's volcanic, thundering body, for Belias and his world—his dark heaven—were the same, each a glittering reflection of the other, a reflection of a reflection, a reflection nested in itself; and if one wished to visualize these moments as Pietro experienced them, one might imagine Athoth, the beautiful aeon Athoth and his club-footed companion Pietro simply walking together. Around them was a darkness so deep and sharp and soul-destroying that the surrounding mountains and cratered ice sheets were simply chiaroscuro contrasts of the same tenebrous void. As Pietro moved through this negative terrain, he imagined that he was looking into (or through) a crystal gazing globe that had been crazed with glittering cracks, so that the darkness

within appeared as shards of black, their various changing shapes defined only by slight differences of darkness and edgings of silver.

The darkness was palpable, tactile, numbing ... (*Shadows* 332–3).

FIGURE 1 *"Pandemonium", from John Milton,* The Paradise Lost, *John Martin, Yale Center for British Art, 1831.*

FIGURE 2 *"Satan Presiding at the Infernal Council", from John Milton,* The Paradise Lost, *John Martin, Victoria and Albert Museum, 1824.*

And herewith is my "plot-map" of Belias's domain, my interpolation/interpretation of Martin's mezzotints into a narrative "plot picture" ("Private Notebook") (see Figures 3–4):

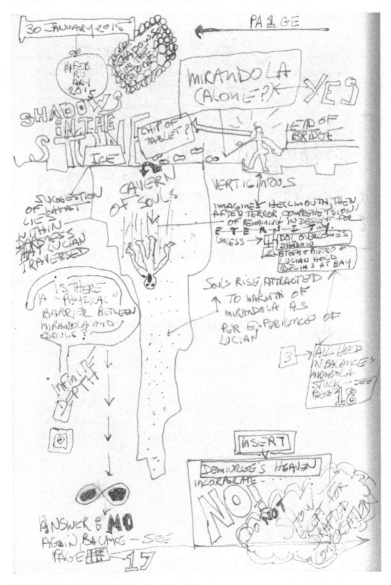

FIGURE 3 *Hand-drawn by the author.*

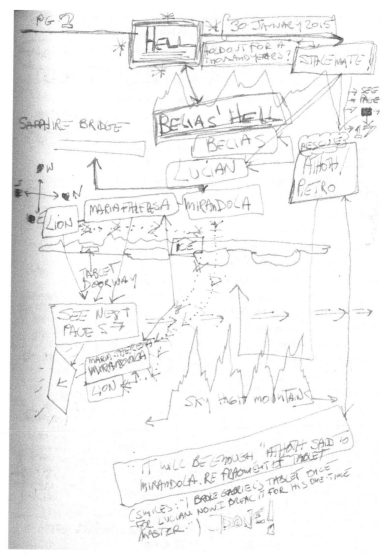

FIGURE 4 *Hand-drawn by the author.*

When I'm "stuck" at a plot juncture, whether the problem is one of determining a creative choice or determining what choices might be possible/available, I often draw my way through the block.

These sketches are a combination of doodle, mind-map, and notes, one of many techniques I use to break through what I think of as "temporary" writer's blocks; and they were the means for working out the intricacies of intersecting plot lines in *Shadows*. The examples above are just a part of a larger map I used to work out and integrate multiple plot lines.

Sketches such as these are often associated with spurts of ongoing research, which is also what I do when I'm "stuck." I agree with Robert McKee when he says:

> You're blocked because you have nothing to say. Your talent didn't abandon you. If you had something to say, you couldn't stop yourself from writing ... Talent must be stimulated by facts and ideas. Do research. Feed your talent. Research not only wins the war on cliché, it's the key to victory over fear and its cousin, depression.
>
> (73–4)

For me research is an ongoing, intervening process as I "discover" (often through the very process of researching) new plot shifts which drive narrative and also help provide the layering that adds depth and verisimilitude to the story.

I might also mention parenthetically that I used the plot arc of *Paradise Lost* as a reference point for *Shadows*, which I referred to from time to time just as a navigator might take bearings from the stars, as I constructed, or rather discovered my story, its particular structure—the various levels of conflict (inner, personal, extra-personal) and progressive complications (McKee 146, 181)—and ideation, by which I mean those story "objects," those grabbing ideas which catalyze new and unexpected plot branchings, some of which profoundly affect the overarching plotline itself.

There were other story objects: these were instigating images, such as airships ... and a hallucinatory dream/vision of a crack in the sky. The crack in the sky seemed to have an almost electrical charge, and its effect on me was something like the catalytic shock of first seeing Martin's mezzotints. I still don't quite understand why this particular image affected me as it did, why it stirred up the dark waters of my unconscious. Perhaps I "recognized" it as one of those archetypal gateways, one of Joseph Campbell's thresholds, that divides the mundane and the nominal (71). Campbell's quote that

"The regions of the unknown ... are free fields for the protection of unconscious content" (72) certainly holds true for me in regard to this image, which I imagined as follows:

> Louisa glimpsed the crack that separated this world or this place from another. It was ebon black; yet as she was whisked through it, as she felt a sudden, deep chill permeate her flesh and bones, she could see into the darkness. It had its own brightness. Its air was thin and difficult to breathe, and the balloon descended, fell as if hydrogen could hold no lift in this place.
>
> (*Shadows* 66)

Louisa, who is to discover she is the reincarnation of a Gnostic deity, passes through the crack in the sky, passes from Virginia circa the Civil War into the aeon Belias' dark heaven [Milton's hell (*Paradise Lost*)] and then into Florence during the height of the Renaissance, into a parallel timeline influenced, unlike our own, by classicism and Gnosticism, a timeline in which humankind had not "evolved" into consciousness in the same way "we" did in our own consensual timeline.

And the vehicle that transfers Louisa through the crack in the sky is a balloon "towed by Louisa's father's ship ... commissioned to transfer the barge—and the fully-inflated twenty-four foot diameter hydrogen balloon tethered to its deck—from the Richmond Gas Works to General Langdon at Chuffin's Bluff" (*Shadows* 79). I believe that the roots of the idea to have Louisa pass through the crack in the sky in a balloon came from a scene from my historical novel *The Silent* (1998). *The Silent*'s protagonist Mundy McDowell had found a book in the haversack of a dead soldier:

> I sat down against the north edge of one of those rocks, and right there in the rain I opened up Eurastus' haversack and took out the book, which had a yellow paper cover and a drawing of a cigar-shaped balloon with an evil looking man with a moustache leaning out of a what looked like a carved wooden basket. But looking at that picture made me feel like I was right in the basket and looking straight down; and there were rods sticking out from all over the basket, and hanging on ropes from the rods were huge globes all lit up; and in the middle of those rods and ropes and globes was a boy who

didn't look to be much older than me hanging from a rope ladder and climbing up to get into the balloon, and way below that was a city that was so far down that the buildings looked like toys. The boy climbing the ladder wore a union uniform and looked real determined, not scared at all. I finished reading that picture for I don't know how long before I read the title called *Private Newton's War in the Air*. Underneath the picture was written "A True Flag Adventure Book by R. A. Riley."

(54)

Much of the research for the scenes that take place in the Civil War parallel timeline in *Shadows* had already been done in preparation for writing *The Silent*, but I resumed researching balloons before I started the chapter in which Louisa, the daughter of light, would escape a bombardment by the Union Army in a balloon. And as I researched balloons, I also, of course, came upon websites describing dirigibles, which led me serendipitously to a Wikipedia entry entitled "Vacuum Airship." To quote the article, "A vacuum airship, also known as a vacuum balloon, is a hypothetical airship that is evacuated rather than filled with a lighter-than-air gas such as hydrogen or helium. First proposed by Italian monk Francesco Lana de Terzi [Lana-Terzi] in 1670, the vacuum balloon would be the ultimate expression of displacement lift power" (para 1). Of course, the problem is that with "a near-vacuum inside the airbag, the atmospheric pressure would exert enormous forces on the airbag, causing it to collapse if not supported. Though it is possible to reinforce the airbag with an internal structure, it is theorized that any structure strong enough to withstand the forces would invariably weigh the vacuum airship down and exceed the total lift capacity of the airship, preventing flight" (par 10). Thus, we would need what engineers wryly refer to as "unobtainium," which Woodward Heflin defined in *Interim Glossary, Aero-Space Terms* as "A substance having the exact high test properties required for a piece of hardware or other item of use, but not obtainable whether because it theoretically cannot exist or because technology is insufficiently advanced to produce it" (qtd. in "Unobtainium"). Perhaps in future, nanotechnology might create a material that could withstand that kind of atmospheric pressure, but when I read a reference to unobtainium on the web, I realized that I already knew of such a (fictional) substance: souls! As I wrote in *Shadows*:

"You have not yet explained what lifts this ship," Louisa said.
"Do you still believe it might be coal gas?" the archbishop asked.
"No, I think not."
"Well, you will soon have the opportunity to ask the captain."
"But I'm asking you."
The archbishop appeared surprised and said, "Be careful,
childe. And be careful when you're on high."
"I shall endeavor to do so."
The archbishop smiled and said, "The envelope that buoys the
ship is filled with ... emptiness, utter emptiness which displaces
the materia of the air itself and thus lifts us. Be mindful of the
membrane that contains the emptiness, for it is an interweaving
of souls; and even accursed souls have more density and
strength than any form of corrupt matter" (145–6).

And as I had already seen Lana-Terzi's vacuum airship referred
to as "Lana's Famous Flying Boat" (MacDonnell) ... and as I was
also rereading Patrick O'Brian's Aubrey/Maturin series of naval
historical novels set in the time of the Napoleonic Wars, I conflated
all this information into a fictional object: I suddenly saw a dirigible
rising over Florence, a dirigible that I visualized as an airborne
version of a seventeenth century Portuguese Nau. Thus I created the
papal airship *Ascensione*, which introduced new plot branchings
and characters. Here is how I envisioned the airship—which I based
on detailed computer graphics I found in a master's thesis by Audrey
Elizabeth Wells—and how I employed a layering of detail to bring
the image to life. Thus the synergy produced by the combination of
research, layering, and extrapolation to create narrative.
    The following is from Louisa's perspective:

As Louisa climbed the rope ladder that was vibrating in
the soot-stinking wind, she looked up at the gondola of the
airship. It was attached to the keel frame of the hull envelope
and was some two hundred feet in length. The envelope above
it was thin and long and didn't look like any balloon Louisa
had ever seen. In fact from below, the gondola looked like the
hull of a carrack with open gun ports. Shrouds were attached
to dead eye blocks fixed to the gondola and the envelope, and
what could only be described as a bowsprit projected from
the front of the gondola. A half-deck was suspended below

and behind the bowsprit, and what looked like retractable masts were fastened to the gondola; their webbed rigging snapped in the wind. Aft was a large triangular lateen sail that could be a rudder. Ropes and stays connected the gondola with the envelope ... and the balloon—if, indeed, that's what it was—was covered with some gauzy material that seemed to shimmer and glow like heated metal ...

The gondola above her was a wooden shadow framed by the glowing nimbus of the airship's balloon envelope. The rope ladder Louisa was climbing disappeared into the main hatch of the gondola; and when she reached it, two rough-looking soldier priests pulled her and then the archbishop onto the deck. The priests wore narrow-brimmed black caps and leather doublets imprinted with the papal insignia: a crimson cross encircled by twisted vines.

"Get them away from the threshold," someone shouted with authority. "And be quick. Others are waiting to ascend."

The soldiers obeyed, although they were clearly awed by Louisa and continued to mumble paternosters and bow their heads before her.

Louisa was also awed as she stood in the center of the huge deck that could have been a quarter-deck if it were not covered. She looked through the dusty air turned golden by shafts of light from the many portholes, gun ports, hatches, and door-sized openings cut into the wooden walls and floor. There were four cannons the size of carronade guns on each side of the deck, and barrels, sacks, and boxes were secured along the bulkheads. Soldiers—which Louisa thought of as sailors—went about their tasks with practiced routine while officers in satin caps, doublets, and open-sided embroidered *guarnacca* tunics shouted orders at them (117–18).

And this from another character's perspective—Lucian ben-Hanania—as he sees the airship from an aerial "bridge" created by the angel Gabriel:

—and felt something warm and moist envelop him.

He had passed through a thin membrane akin to the crack in the sky that the Daughter of Light had traversed. In an instant, he passed from pitch dark into familiar night: immoveable stars flickered in their panoply, cool erratic breezes spun past him as did moist swirls of cloud, and beneath his feet and extending through the elevated atmosphere was the narrow span of the sapphire bridge; its light was now strong and steady ... and Lucian could see the bridge's terminus: the huge, golden-sailed airship that carried the Daughter of Light, Isabella, and the aeon Athoth. Above the gondola hull with its projecting masts, sails, and webbed rigging—with its own constellations of gun ports and hatches that leaked the soft buttery light of habitation—was an envelope that radiated its own soft iridescence. The envelope glowed with the same light as the bridge, the same light as the souls that had been swallowed in the universe he left behind. But the bridge seemed to end somewhere short of the hull, just above what might be identified as a mizzen topsail, except its mast extended horizontally from the hull rather than vertically from the deck. Lucian noticed that the airship was moving, occluding the stars behind it, and the bridge span moved in perfect harmony with the ship. As he stepped carefully to the end of the bridge's span, he felt that he was being watched. He crouched low, balancing, calculating whether he could catch one of the shrouds or ratlines creaking and singing through the air below him; and as he surveyed the ship, he spied a partially open hatchway and wondered when an unseen lookout would notice him and sound the alarm; but there was nothing for it: he couldn't go back, only forward. But what about the tablet, Gabriel's key ... the bridge?.

He kneeled and touched the edges of the span to balance himself; as he did so, the bridge simply ceased to be, or, rather, was transmogrified, and Lucian found himself clutching what was now a small sapphire tablet, and falling (167–8).

Lastly, the scene below of a meeting with the high order angel who is the captain of the airship is an example of the effects the dirigible's envelope (airbag) of souls would have upon Lucian. This might also be considered as another example of how research drives narrative, layering ... and extrapolation:

Rudolfo led Lucian toward a bright coruscation of light at the end of a long, wide corridor. They walked past a series of staterooms and high cladded doors marked with the Pope's insignia of twisted vines encircling a cross and the single word

PROIBITO stamped in red. Blue-tinged light pierced through ceiling grates, hatches, and mirrored portholes cut at angles high in the walls. Dust sparkled then disappeared into ever fading blue shadows ... blue, the blue of souls, the blue of Gabriel's tablet ...

The eunuch stopped before a steep companionway bathed in iridescent light. The hatch was open at the top of the narrow staircase.

The captain awaits you.

Lucian looked up into the bleaching, eye-aching light above.

"Has the daughter of light told you about the boundary?" Rudolfo asked, his eyes averted from the watery light.

"Yes, she told me of the boundary ... of the accursed souls that lift this accused ship" ...

Lucian heard soft laughter from above; he tried to look up as he climbed, but the light was too bright. As soon as he reached the landing, he felt the crushing pressure of the lost souls trapped above him. He was suddenly weak, dizzy, and disoriented; and if the aeon had not grasped his arm at just that moment, Lucian would have fallen backwards down the staircase. Nevertheless, he resisted the aeon.

"Welcome, young theurgist," the aeon said, holding him even tighter. As he spoke the dazzling light became bearable; and Lucian could make out his kindly features: soft yet piercing eyes, a prominent aquiline nose, and a full, generous mouth, all of which gave him a regal, almost handsome appearance despite his slight double chin and fleshy girth. He wore a velvet cap, damask doublet, and a gold-fringed tunic.

"You do not appear as I remember," Lucian said, still trying to pull away from the aeon. He tasted angry bile, the black bile of hatred. The aeon released him; but this place—the lost souls above, the noxious, enervating aethers that swirled around him like motes of dust caught in unblinking light— seemed to be sucking away all his strength, his very life-force. He stumbled backward again. The aeon smiled and caught him: this time Lucian did not—could not—resist.

"Shall I raise the temperature?" asked the aeon.

"I'm sure I do not understand," Lucian said weakly. He wanted to put out the aeon's eyes, pull the flesh from his soft face (if flesh it was), but the enervating aethers radiating from the lost souls trapped in the airship's envelope swallowed Lucian's anger, grief, and hatred.

"The poor, denuded souls above are as cold as darkness itself," the aeon said, "and you—sweet, angry childe of light—you are too warm. You radiate the very heat of life itself, and they can do naught but try to take nourishment for themselves."

"Is that why you summoned me?" Lucian asked. "To murder me here because you neglected to do so when you executed my parents?" As the aeon caressed his face, Lucian felt a permeating warmth ... and strength.

Revolted by his own feelings, he pulled away from the aeon's touch.

Would you prefer to lean against the balustrade rail for support?

Lucian nodded.

The temperature was indeed rising, and as it did so, the light dimmed ... clarified. Now he could see the vast expanses of decking, which looked as dry and brittle as autumn leaves. Iron rails seemed to define the long, narrowing perspective lines, and they, like the scattered stores of armor and cannon, were all pitted and coated with rust (188–90).

As might be surmised by the preceding excerpts and analysis of *Shadows*, the embracing concepts of research driving and creating narrative, story worlds functioning as character, and layering as technique are intertwined. They work together, both as conscious and unconscious practice, and, in fact, constitute both continuing practice and result. By "result," I refer to the concept of story worlds functioning as characters: if I've accomplished what I set out to do in this novel, the story worlds of Florence with its catacombs, Venice with its Pope, angels existing simultaneously as beings and places, the aerial bridge and its manifestations, and the soul-powered airship should all function as narrative drivers and have the positive valence of the story's human and supernatural characters.

##

8

A Very Few Last Words about ... You

We writers yearn for cookie-patterns, for a "just do this and all will be well". Unfortunately, it usually doesn't work that way. Writers approach their craft in such individual ways that no craft lesson plan fits all. When I'm conducting writers' workshops, I tell the participants that if my advice sounds deadeningly wrong to you, that just means that I'm not the one to help you to hone your craft ... that I'm not in synch with the way you conceptualize story and its architecture. Some writers are plot-oriented, others not; some writers outline scene by scene, others just start writing. Some writers start writing the end of the story first, some start in the middle; I have to start at the beginning and "learn" about my characters, settings, and unforeseen subplots as I go. Then I periodically review what I've written and refit, add details to enhance depth of character, strengthen intersecting plotlines, and insert the all important clues that I will pay off later.

There seem to be as many approaches to the craft of writing as there are writers, and novice writers searching for help need to keep searching until they find the writers/tutors/instructors who have mindsets simpatico with their own. At the end of a workshop, *maybe* one or two out of ten or twenty participants will come over to tell me how excited they are that I've focused their understanding of exactly what they need to do. I consider that a success!

Of course, I would hope that you're one of those readers whom I "speak to," the one or two or one hundred who experience a sort of craft novum, who immediately sense how it can all work. But it really doesn't matter if your mindset isn't simpatico with mine because the concepts in this counterfactual toolbox aren't dependent on your writing style, creative process, likes, dislikes, personality ... or your position about the nature of history and morality and choice. They are simply tools that can be successfully employed by any practitioner who is familiar with the counterfactual fiction genre and the craft of writing.

I wish you every success in your journeys into alternity, and I look forward to reading your counterfactual chronicles of unseen pasts and altered presents.

###

BIBLIOGRAPHY

Agrippa von Nettesheim, Heinrich Cornelius. *Three Books of Occult Philosophy*. Ed. Donald Tyson. Trans. James Freake. St. Paul: Llewellyn, 1993. Print.

Aldiss, Brian Wilson. *The Malacia Tapestry*. New York: Harper, 1977. Print.

Alkon, Paul. "Alternate History and Postmodern Temporality." *Time, Literature and the Arts: Essays in Honor of Samuel L. Macey*. Ed. Thomas R. Cleary. U of Victoria, 1994. 65–85.

Amis, Kingsley. *The Alteration*. London: Carroll, 1988. Print.

Anders, Charlie Jane. "How Many Definitions of Science Fiction Are There?" *Io9*, Aug. 2, 2010, http://io9.com/5622186/how-many-defintions-of-science-fiction-are-there.

Anderson, Poul. *The Time Patrol*. New York: T. Doherty Associates, 1991. Print. Time Patrol 1–4 Omnibus.

Asimov, Isaac. "Foundation." *The Foundation Trilogy*. Book Club. New York: Doubleday, 1951. 1–227. Print.

"Asimov's Encyclopedia Galactica." *World Heritage Encyclopedia*. N.p, 2014. Web. 13 Sept. 2015.

Austen, Jane. *Pride and Prejudice*. New York: Penguin Books, 2003.

Binet, Laurent. *Civilizations*. Trans. Sam Taylor. New York: Farrar, 2021. Print.

Birmingham, John. *He Died with a Felafel in His Hand*. Duffy & Snellgrove, 2001. *Open WorldCat*, http://catalog.hathitrust.org/api/volumes/oclc/48954284.html.

Birmingham, John. *Weapons of Choice*. 1st ed. New York: Del Rey/Ballantine Books, 2004.

Birmingham, John. *Without Warning*. Pan Macmillan Australia, 2008.

Bishop, Michael. *Count Geiger's Blues: A Comedy*. 1st ed. New York: T. Doherty Associates, 1992.

Bishop, Michael. *The Quickening*. Eugene, OR: Pulphouse, 1991.

Bishop, Michael. "Rogue Tomato." *New Dimensions 5*. Ed. Robert Silverberg. New York: Harper & Row, 1975. Print.

Bishop, Michael. *The Secret Ascension: Philip K. Dick Is Dead, Alas.* New York: Tor, 1987.

Bishop, Michael. *Unicorn Mountain.* 1st ed. Arbor House: Morrow, 1988.

Bisson, Terry. *Any Day Now.* New York: Overlook, 2012.

Bisson, Terry. *Fire on the Mountain.* Oakland, CA: PM, 2009. Print.

Broderick, Damien. "Novum." *The Encyclopedia of Science Fiction.* Gollancz, Apr. 2, 2015. Web. Sept. 12, 2015.

Browne, Thomas Sir. *Religio Medici, Hydriotaphia, and the Letter to a Friend.* London: S. Low, 1880. *Project Gutenberg.* Web. Nov. 8, 2015.

Brunner, John. *The Sheep Look Up.* New York: Ballatine, 1973. Print.

Bruno, Giordano. *Gli Eroici Furori.* Vol. 1. Trans. L. Williams. Prod. Sjaani, Ted Garvin et al. *Project Gutenberg.* N.p., 2006. Web. Sept. 20, 2015.

Buckland, Corinne. "Transcendent History: Markus Zusak's The Book Thief." *Exploring the Benefits of the Alternate History Genre = W Poszukiwaniu Pożyteczności Gatunku Historii Alternatywnych.* Ed. Zdzisław Wąsik, Marek Oziewicz and Deszcz-Tryhubczak. Wroclaw: Wroclaw Publ, 2011. 71–81. Print.

Byatt, A. S. *Possession: A Romance,* vol. 1. Vintage internat. ed. New York: Vintage Books, 1991.

Byatt, A. S. "Quote." *The Complete Aubrey/Maturin Novels.* Vol. 3. New York: Norton, 2004. inside flap jacket. Print.

Carlyle, Thomas. *On Heroes, Hero-Worship, and the Heroic in History.* London: James Fraser, 1841. *Project Gutenberg.* Web. Oct. 3, 2015.

Cosma, Ioana. *Angels in-between: The Poetics of Excess and the Crisis of Representation.* Diss. U of Toronto, 2009. Print.

Chabon, Michael. *The Yiddish Policemen's Union: A Novel.* New York: HarperCollins, 2007. Print.

Chamberlain, Gordon B. "Afterword: Allohistory in Science Fiction." *Eleven Stories of the World as It Might Have Been.* Ed. Charles Waugh and Martin Harry Greenberg. New York: Garland, 1986. 281–300. Print.

Chapman, Edgar L. "'Three Stages of Alternate History Fiction and the "Metaphysical If".' Introduction." *Classic and Iconoclastic Alternate History Science Fiction.* Ed. Chapman and Carl B. Yolk. Lampeter: Mellen, 2003. 1–27. Print.

Cheney, Margaret. *Tesla: Man out of Time.* Mattituck: Amereon, 1998. Print.

Clark, P. Djèlí. *A Master of Djinn.* 1st ed. New York: Tom Doherty Associates Book, 2021.

Crowley, John. *Aegypt.* New York: Bantam Books, 1987.

Crowley, John. *Four Freedoms.* 1st ed. New York: William Morrow, 2009.

Crowley, John. *Great Work of Time.* New York: Bantam Books, 1991.

Dann, Jack. "Da Vinci Rising." *Isaac Asimov's Science Fiction Magazine*, vol. 19, no. 6, May 1995. 116–66.

Dann, Jack. *The Fiction Writer's Guide to Alternate History: A Handbook on Craft, Art, and History*. London: Bloomsbury, 2023. Print.

Dann, Jack. "The Memory Cathedral: Eros, Magic and Myth." *The Fantastic Self: Essays on the Subject of the Self*. Ed. Janeen Webb and Andrew Enstice. North Perth: Eidolon, 1999. 10–18. Print.

Dann, Jack. *The Memory Cathedral: A Secret History of Leonardo Da Vinci*. New York: Bantam, 1995. Print.

Dann, Jack. "Private Notebook." 2012–21: n. pag. Print.

Dann, Jack. "A Note from Jack Dann." *The Silent*. New York: Bantam, 1998. 283–6. Print.

Dann, Jack. *Promised Land: Stories of Another America*. Hornsea: PS, 2007. Print.

Dann, Jack. *The Rebel: An Imagined Life of James Dean*. New York: Morrow, 2004. Print.

Dann, Jack. *The Rebel: Second Chance*. Foster: Satalyte, 2015. Print.

Dann, Jack. *Shadows in the Stone: A Book of Transformations*. Melbourne: IFWG Publishing Australia, 2019. Print.

Dann, Jack. *The Silent*. New York: Bantam, 1998. Print.

Dann, Jack, Gardner Dozois and Michael Swanwick. "The Gods of Mars." *Omni*, vol. 7, no. 6, Mar. 1985.

De Camp, L. Sprague. "Aristotle and the Gun." *Futures Past*. Ed. Jack Dann and Gardner Dozois. New York: Ace, 2006. 2–40. Print.

De Camp, L. Sprague. *Lest Darkness Fall*. New York: Holt, 1941. Print.

Dee, John. *John Dee's Five Books of Mystery: Original Sourcebook of Enochian Magic: From the Collected Works Known as Mysteriorum Libri Quinque*. Ed. Joseph H. Peterson. Boston: Weiser, 2003. Print.

Dee, John, Meric Casaubon and Edward Kelly. *Dr. John Dee's Action with Spirits: A True & Faithful Relation of What Paffed for Many Yeers between Dr. John Dee (a Mathematician of Great Fame in Q. Eliz. and King James Their Reignes) and Some Spirits: Tending (Had It Succeeded) to a General Alteration of Moft States and Kingdomes in the World*. 2nd ed. London: Redwood, 1974. Print.

Deighton, Len. *SS-GB: Nazi-Occupied Britain, 1941: A Novel*. New York: Ballantine, 1978. Print.

Di Filippo, Paul. *Murder in Geektopia: Short Story*. Toronto: ChiZine Publications, 2014. *Open WorldCat*, https://www.overdrive.com/search?q=84613DC7-DA05-4FC7-BE5D-A7FD45966C97.

Dick, Philip K. *The Man in the High Castle*. New York: Putnam, 1962. Print.

Disraeli, Benjamin. The *Wondrous Tale of Alroy. The Rise of Iskander.* London: Saunders and Otly, 1833. Internet Archive. Web. Nov. 4, 2015.

Farmer, Philip Jose. "Sail on! Sail on." *A Century of Science Fiction.* Ed. Damon Knight. New York: Simon, 1962. 64–72. Print.

Ferguson, Niall. "Virtual History: Towards a 'Chaotic' Theory of the Past." *Virtual History: Alternatives and Counterfactuals.* Ed. Niall Ferguson. London: Pan, 2003. 1–90. Print.

Fry, Stephen. *Making History.* London: Hutchinson, 1996. Print.

Gibson, William and Bruce Sterling. *The Difference Engine.* New York: Bantam, 1992. Print.

Gingrich, Newt, William R. Forstchen and Albert S. Hanser. *1945.* New York: Baen, 1995. Print.

Golding, William. *Lord of the Flies: A Novel.* New York: Perigee, 1954. Print.

Goldstein, Lisa. "Paradise Is a Walled Garden." *Asimov's Science Fiction,* vol. 35, no. 8, Aug. 2011.

Harland, Richard. *Liberator.* 1st ed. New York: Simon & Schuster BFYR, 2012.

Harland, Richard. *Song of the Slums.* Sydney, Australia: Allen & Unwin, 2013.

Harland, Richard. *Worldshaker.* Sydney, Australia: Allen & Unwin, 2009.

Harris, Robert. *Fatherland.* London: BCA, 1992. Print.

Heinlein, Robert. *Beyond This Horizon.* New York: Signet, 1975. Print.

Hellekson, Karen. *The Alternate History: Refiguring Historical Time.* Kent, OH: Kent State UP, 2001.

Howe, Irving. *A Critic's Notebook.* Ed. Nicholas Howe. San Diego: Harcourt, 1995. Print.

墨客, hunxi. "Rewriting the Tradition: Destiny and Diaspora in Shelley Parker-Chan's *She Who Became the Sun.*" *Tor.com,* Aug. 4, 2021, https://www.tor.com/2021/08/04/destiny-and-diaspora-in-shelley-parker-chans-she-who-became-the-sun/.

James, Edward. *Science Fiction in the Twentieth Century.* Oxford: Oxford UP, 1994. Print.

Jaynes, Julian. *The Origin of Consciousness in the Breakdown of the Bicameral Mind.* Boston: Houghton, 1976. Print.

Jason777. "Alternate History FAQ." *Alternate History Wiki.* N.p., Nov. 2, 2012. Web. Nov. 8, 2015. <http://wiki.alternatehistory.com/doku.php/alternate_history_faq>.

Kessel, John. "Buffalo." *The Magazine of Fantasy & Science Fiction,* vol. 80, no. 1, Jan. 1991.

Kessel, John. "The Invisible Empire." *Conjunctions: 39, The New Wave Fabulists.* Ed. Bradford Morrow and Peter Straub. Annandale-on-Hudson: Bard, 2002. Print.

Kessel, John. *Pride and Prometheus.* 1st ed. New York: Saga Press, 2018.

Kessel, John. "Remaking History: The Short Fiction." *Kim Stanley Robinson Maps the Unimaginable: Critical Essays.* Ed. William

J. Burling. Jefferson: McFarland, 2009. 83–94. Print. Critical Explorations in Science Fiction and Fantasy 13.

King, Stephen. *11/22/63: A Novel*. New York: Scribner, 2011. Print.

Knight, Damon. *In Search of Wonder*. 2nd ed. Chicago: Advent, 1967.

Kosinski, Jerzy. *The Painted Bird*. 2nd ed. Boston: Houghton, 1976. Print.

Kowal, Mary Robinette. *The Calculating Stars*. 1st ed. New York: Tor, a Tom Doherty Associates Books, 2018.

Lana-Terzi, Francesco. *The Aerial Ship*. Ed. Thomas O'Brien Hubbard and John Henry Ledeboer. London: King, 1910. Print.

L'Engle, Madeleine. "9 Thoughts on Writing by Madeleine L'Engle." Scribblepreach.com. *Scribblepreach*. N.p., n.d. Web. Sept. 20, 2015.

Lebow, Richard Ned. "Counterfactual Thought Experiments: A Necessary Teaching Tool." *The History Teacher*, vol. 40, no. 2 (2007): 153–76. *JSTOR*. Web. Sept. 5, 2013.

Leinster, Murray. "Sideways in Time." *Before the Golden Age*. Ed. Isaac Asimov. Garden City: Doubleday, 1974. 496–540. Print.

MacDonnell, Joseph S. J. "Francesco Lana-Terzi, S.J. (1631–1687): The Father of Aeronautics." N.p., n.d. Web. Nov. 3, 2015.

Malzberg, Barry N. "Fugato." *Alternate Warriors*, Ed. Michael D. Resnick, 1st ed. New York: Tor, 1993.

Malzberg, Barry N. "Heavy Metal." *Alternate Presidents*, Ed. Michael D. Resnick, 1st ed. New York: Tom Doherty Associates, 1992.

Malzberg, Barry N. "In the Stone House." *In the Stone House*, 1st ed. Sauk City, WI: Arkham House Publishers, 2000.

Martin, John. *Paradise Lost—Pandemonium*. 1824. Mezzotint. British Museum. *The History of Hell*. Alice K. Turner. San Diegllo: Harcourt, 1995. N.pag (inserted between 186–8). Print. *Dark Classics*. Web. Oct. 29, 2015. <http://darkclassics.blogspot.com.au/p/john-martin-paradise-lost.html>.

Martin, John. *Paradise Lost—Satan Presiding at the Infernal Council*. 1824. Mezzotint. Nat. Gallery of Canada. *History of Hell*. Alice K. Turner. San Diego: Harcourt, 1995. N.pag (inserted between 186–8). Print. *Dark Classics*. Web. Oct. 29, 2015. <http://darkclassics.blogspot.com.au/p/johnmartinparadiselost.html>.

McKee, Robert. *Story: Substance, Structure, Style and the Principles of Screenwriting*. New York: ReganBooks, 1997. Print.

McIntyre, Vonda N. "Pitfall #1: The Expository Lump." *Pitfalls of Writing Science Fiction & Fantasy, General Useful Information, & Other Opinionated Comments*. N.p., Sept. 8, 2003. Web. Sept. 13, 2015.

Meyer, Marvin, ed. "The Secret Book of John." *The Gnostic Gospels: The Sacred Writings of the Nag Hammadi Library, the Berlin Gnostic Codex and Codex Tchacos*. Trans. Marvin Meyer. London: Folio, 2007. 85–109. Print.

Milton, John. "Paradise Lost." *Milton Poetical Works*. Ed. Douglas Bush. London: Oxford UP, 1969. 201–462. Print.

Myer, Marvin and Elaine Pagels, eds. *The Gnostic Gospels: The Sacred Writings of the Nag Hammadi Library, The Berlin Gnostic Codex and the Codex Tchacos*. London.

Moore, Ward. *Bring the Jubilee*. New York: Ballantine, 1953. Print.

Nabokov, Vladimir. *Ada, or Ardor: A Family Chronicle*. New York: McGraw, 1969. Print.

Nevins, Jess. "Prescriptivists vs. Descriptivists: Defining Steampunk." *Science Fiction Studies*, vol. 38, no. 3 (2011): 513–18. Print.

Newitz, Annalee. *The Future of Another Timeline*. New York: Tor, 2019. Print.

Newman, Kim. *Anno-Dracula*. New York: Simon & Schuster, 1992. Print. Anno Dracula Series. Vol. 1 of 6. 1992–2015.

Nguyen, Phong. *Pages from the Textbook of Alternate History*. Plano, TX: Queen's Ferry Press, 2014.

Nguyen, Phong. "Research Notes: Pages from the Textbook of Alternate History." *Necessary Fiction*. N.p., Jan. 17, 2004. Web. Sept. 23, 2015.

Nicholls, Peter, and David Langford. "Steampunk." *The Encyclopedia of Science Fiction*, Gollancz, Apr. 22, 2015, http://www.sfencyclopedia. com/entry/steampunk.

O'Brian, Patrick. *The Complete Aubrey/Maturin Novels*, vol. 5, New York: Norton, 2004. Print.

Parker-Chan, Shelley. *She Who Became the Sun*. London: Mantle, 2021.

Priest, Christopher. *The Adjacent*. London: Gollancz, 2013.

Priest, Christopher. *The Islanders*. London: Gollancz, 2011.

Priest, Christopher. *The Separation*. London: Simon & Schuster, 2001.

Ransom, Amy J. "Warping Time: Alternate History, Historical Fantasy, and the Postmodern Uchronie Québécoise." *Extrapolation*, vol. 51, no. 2 (2010): 258–80. Print.

Robinson, Kim Stanley. "Introduction." *Promised Land: Stories of Another America. By Jack Dann*. First: PS Publishing, 2007. vii–xiv.

Robinson, Kim Stanley. "Notes for an Essay on Cecelia Holland." *Foundation*, vol. 40 (1987): 54–61. Print.

Robinson, Kim Stanley. "The Lucky Strike." *Universe 14*. Ed. Terry Carr. New York: Doubleday, 1984. Print.

Roberts, Keith. *Pavane*. New York: Ace, 1968. Print.

Robinson, Kim Stanley. "A Sensitive Dependence on Initial Conditions." *A Sensitive Dependence on Initial Conditions*. Eugene, OR: Pulphouse Publishing, 1991. 1–19, http://www.baenebooks.com/ chapters/1597801844/1597801844___6.htm.

Robinson, Kim Stanley. *The Years of Rice and Salt*. New York: Bantam, 2003. Print.

Robinson, Kim Stanley. "Vinland the Dream." *Isaac Asimov's Science Fiction Magazine*, vol. 15, no. 12 & 13, Nov. 1991.

Rosenfeld, Gavriel D. "Why Do We Ask 'What If?' Reflections on the Function of Alternate History." *History and Theory*, vol. 41, no. 4, Theme Issue 41: Unconventional History (2002): 90–103. Print.

Rosenfeld, Gavriel D. *The World Hitler Never Made: Alternate History and the Memory of Nazism*. Cambridge UP, 2005. Print.

Roth, Philip. *The Plot against America: [a Novel]*. London: Cape, 2004. Print.

Russ, Joanna. "The Wearing Out of Genre Materials." *College English*, vol. 33, no. 1 (1971): 46–54. Print.

Salinger, Jerome D. *The Catcher in the Rye*. Boston: Little, 1991. Print.

Sanford, Maggie Ryan. "AC/DC: The Tesla–Edison Feud." *Mental Floss*. N.p., Jul. 10, 2012. Web. Sept. 4, 2015.

Sargent, Pamela. *Climb the Wind: A Novel of Another North America*. New York: HarperPrism, 1999. Print.

Sargent, Pamela. *Hillary Orbits Venus. Fictionwise*. Jul. 2007. Web.

Sargent, Pamela. *Ruler of the Sky: A Novel of Genghis Khan*. 1st American ed. New York: Crown Publishers, 1993.

Sargent, Pamela. "Science Fiction, Historical Fiction, and Alternative History." *The Bulletin of the Science Fiction and Fantasy Writers of America*, vol. 29, Fall, 1995.

Sargent, Pamela. "The Sleeping Serpent." *Amazing Stories*, vol. 66, no. 9, Jan. 1992.

Schmunk, Robert B. "Introduction: What Is Alternate History?" *Uchronia: The Alternate History List*. N.p., n.d. Web. Nov. 4, 2015.

Schmunk, Robert B. "Sidewise Awards for Alternate History." *Uchronia: The Alternate History List*. N.p., n.d. Web. Nov. 8, 2015.

Schmunk, Robert B. "Welcome to Uchronia: The Alternate History List." *Uchronia: The Alternate History List*. N.p., n.d. Web. Nov. 4, 2015.

Schneider-Mayerson. "What Almost Was: The Politics of the Contemporary Alternate History Novel." *American Studies*, vol. 50, no. 3 & 4, Fall/Winter 2009. 63–83.

Sedia, Ekaterina. "Challenges of Writing Alternate History Set in Other Cultures." *Tor.com*. TOR, Oct. 4, 2011. Web. Sept. 10, 2015. <http://www.tor.com/2011/10/04/alternate-history-in-other-cultures/>

Sedia, Ekaterina. *Heart of Iron*. Rockville: Prime, 2011. Print.

Shawl, Nisi. *Everfair*. 1st ed. New York: TOR, 2016.

Shelley, Mary Wollstonecraft. *Frankenstein, or, The Modern Prometheus*. Rev. ed. London; New York: Penguin Books, 2003.

Shiner, Lewis. *Collected Stories*. Burton: Subterranean, 2009 Print.

Shiner, Lewis. "The Death of Che Guevara." *Subterranean Online*, Nov. 2009. Web.

Shiner, Lewis. *Glimpses*. 1st ed. W. Morrow, 1993.

Shiner, Lewis. "Primes." *The Magazine of Fantasy & Science Fiction*, vol. 99, no. 4 & 5, Oct. 2000.

Shiner, Lewis. "Twilight Time." *Isaac Asimov's Science Fiction Magazine*, vol. 8, no. 4, Apr. 1984.

Shiner, Lewis. "White City." *Isaac Asimov's Science Fiction Magazine*, vol. 14, no. 6, June 1990.

Shippey, Tom. "Alternate Historians: Newt, Kingers, Harry, and Me." *Journal of the Fantastic in the Arts,* vol. 8 (1996): 15–33. Print.

Shirrefs, Mark and John Thomson. *Spellbinder*. Dir. Noel Price. 26 Episodes. Nine Network (Film Australia) and Telewizja Polska (Poland) 1995. Television.

Spinrad, Norman. *The Iron Dream*. New York: Avon, 1972. Print.

Stableford, Brian M. and David Langford. "Parallel Worlds." *The Encyclopedia of Science Fiction*. Gollancz, June 24, 2014. Web. Aug. 14, 2015.

Sterling, Bruce. "Dori Bangs." *Isaac Asimov's Science Fiction Magazine*, vol. 13, no. 7, Sept., 1989.

Sterling, Bruce, and Lewis Shiner. "Mozart in Mirrorshades." *Omni*, vol. 7, no. 12, Sept., 1985.

Swanwick, Michael. *Jack Faust*. New York: Avon, 1997. Print.

Tidhar, Lavie. *Unholy Land*. San Francisco: Tachyon Publications, 2018. Print.

Turtledove, Harry. *Guns of the South*. New York: Del Rey, 1992. Print.

Turtledove, Harry. *The House That George Built: A Tor.Com Original*. Tor, 2009. Open WorldCat, https://www.overdrive.com/search?q=2C2B62DC-9A3B-4EE1-93F0-BB8A689CB508.

Turtledove, Harry. "The How-to of What Might Have Been." *Writers Workshop of Science Fiction & Fantasy*. Ed. Michael Knost. Lexington, KY: Seventh Star Press, 2013.

Twain, Mark. *Adventures of Huckleberry Finn (Tom Sawyer's Comrade)*. New York: C. L. Webster, 1885. Internet Archive, http://archive.org/details/adventureshuckle00twaiiala.

Twain, Mark. *A Connecticut Yankee in King Arthur's Court*. New York: Signet, 2004. Print.

"Unobtainium." *Wikipedia, the Free Encyclopedia*, Oct. 19, 2015. *Wikipedia*, https://en.wikipedia.org/w/index.php?title=Unobtainium&oldid=686526116.

"Unobtainium." *World Wide Words*. N.p., n.d. Web. Nov. 3, 2015.

Urth, Robert. "Tesla Master of Lightning." *Tesla Life and Legacy—War of the Currents*. N.p., n.d. Web. Sept. 4, 2015.

"Vacuum Airship." *Wikipedia, the Free Encyclopedia* Sept. 28, 2015. Wikipedia. Web. Nov. 3, 2015.

Vallentin, Antonina. *Leonardo Da Vinci: The Tragic Pursuit of Perfection*. Trans. E. W. Dikes. New York: Viking, 1938. Print.

Van Nostrand, Albert. *The Denatured Novel*. Indianapolis and New York: Bobs-Merrill, 1960. Print.

Vasari, Giorgio. [*Siege of Florence*]. N.d. Fresco. Palazzo Vecchio. *Florence: the Golden Age 1138–1737*. Gene Adam Bruckner. New York: Abbeville P, 1984. 18–19. Print.

Waldrop, Howard. *A Better World's in Birth!*. Urbana: Golden Gryphon Press, 2003. Print.

Waldrop, Howard. "Calling Your Name." *Stars: Original Stories Based on the Songs of Janis Ian*. Ed. Janis Ian and Mike Resnick. New York: DAW Books, 2003. Print.

Waldrop, Howard. "Hoover's Men." *Omni*, vol. 11, no. 1, Oct. 1988.

Waldrop, Howard. "The Horse of a Different Color (That You Rode in On)." *Scifi.Com*, Nov. 2, 2005. Web.

Waldrop, Howard. "Ike at the Mike." *Omni*, vol. 4, no. 9, June 1982.

Waldrop, Howard. "The Lions Are Asleep This Night." *Omni*, vol. 8, no. 11, Aug. 1986.

Waldrop, Howard. "The World, as We Know't." *Howard Who? Twelve Outstanding Stories of Speculative Fiction*. Ed. Howard Waldrop. 1st ed. New York: Doubleday, 1986.

Webb, Janeen. "Manifest Destiny." *Baggage*. Ed. Gillian Polack. Culcain: Australia, 2010.

Webb, Janeen, and Andrew Enstice. *The Five Star Republic: City of the Sun: Book One*. Australia: IFWG Publishing, 2021.

Wells, Audrey Elizabeth. "Virtual Reconstruction of a Seventeenth-Century Portuguese Nau." MS Thesis. Texas A&M, 2008. Web. Nov. 3, 2015.

White, Hayden V. *Metahistory: The Historical Imagination in Nineteenth-Century Europe*. Fortieth-Anniversary edition. Johns Hopkins UP, 2014.

Williamson, Jack. *The Legion of Time*. Reading: Fantasy P, 1952. Print.

Wolfe, Gary K. and David Langford. "Alternate History." *The Encyclopedia of Science Fiction*. Ed. John Clute, David Langford, Peter Nicholls and Graham Sleight. London: Gollancz, Jul. 24, 2015. Web. July 28, 2015. <http://www.sf-encyclopedia.com/entry/alternate_history>, 2015.

Zebrowski, George. "Lenin in Odessa." *What Might Have Been? Vol II: Alternate Heroes*. Ed. Gregory Benford and Martin Greenberg. New York: Bantam Spectra, 1990. Print.

Zebrowski, George. *Stranger Suns*. New York: Bantam Books, 1991.

THE AUTHOR

Photo credit: Robert Hoge.

Jack Dann has written or edited over eighty books, including the international bestseller *The Memory Cathedral*, *The Rebel*, *The Silent*, *Junction*, and *The Man Who Melted*. He is a recipient of the Nebula Award, the World Fantasy Award (twice), the Australian Aurealis Award (three times), the Ditmar Award (five times), the Australian Shadows Award (for nonfiction), the Peter McNamara Achievement Award and also the Peter McNamara Covenors' Award for Excellence, the Shirley Jackson Award, and the *Premios Gilgames de Narrativa Fantastica* award. He has also been honored by the Mark Twain Society (Esteemed Knight).

His work has been compared to Jorge Luis Borges, Roald Dahl, Lewis Carroll, Castaneda, Ray Bradbury, J. G. Ballard, Mark Twain, and Philip K. Dick. Philip K. Dick, author of the stories from which the films *Blade Runner* and *Total Recall* were made, wrote that *"Junction* is where Ursula Le Guin's *Lathe of Heaven* and Tony Boucher's 'The Quest for Saint Aquin' meet ... and yet it's an entirely new novel .... I may very well be basing some of my future work on *Junction*."

Library Journal has called Dann " ... a true poet who can create pictures with a few perfect words." Roger Zelazny thought he was a reality magician and *Best Sellers* has said that "Jack Dann is a mind-warlock whose magicks will confound, disorient, shock, and delight." *The Washington Post Book World* compared his novel *The*

Man Who Melted with Ingmar Bergman's film *The Seventh Seal*. And Morgan Llwelyn called *The Memory Cathedral*—Dann's novel about Leonardo da Vinci—"a book to cherish, a validation of the novelist's art and fully worthy of its extraordinary subject. I can only say Bravo!"

Dr. Dann is an Adjunct Senior Research Fellow in the School of Communication and Arts at the University of Queensland. He is the author of a number of short story collections. *Booklist* called his collection *Jubilee* "Literary SF of the best sort" and recommended "lay(ing) in extra copies to accommodate readers taking it slowly and luxuriously." In her introduction to his short story collection *Concentration*, critic and scholar Marleen Barr wrote: "Dann is a Faulkner and a Márquez for Jews. His fantastic retellings of the horror stories Nazis made real are more truth than fantasy."

His latest collection is a volume in the *Masters of Science Fiction* series; and his latest novel is *Shadows in the Stone: a Book of Transformations. New York Times* bestselling author Kim Stanley Robinson called it "such a complete world that Italian history no longer seems comprehensible without his cosmic battle of spiritual entities behind and within every historical actor and event."

Jack lives in Australia on a farm overlooking the sea. You can visit his website at [www.jackdann.com] and follow him on Twitter [@ jackmdann] and Facebook [www.facebook.com/jack.dann2].

ROUNDTABLE Q & A CONTRIBUTORS

John Birmingham is a British-Australian author whose work has appeared in *Rolling Stone*, *Playboy*, *Quarterly Essay*, and *The Monthly*. His memoir *He Died with a Falafel in His Hand* has been turned into a play, film, and a graphic novel. His book *Leviathan: the unauthorised biography of Sydney* won Australia's National Prize for Non-Fiction. The Sydney Theater Company created a play based on the book. His novels include the following series: *Axis of Time*, *Disappearance*, *Dave vs. the Monsters*, *A Girl in Time*, and *The Cruel Stars*.

Michael Bishop has written over thirty books and has created what has been called a "body of work that stands among the most admired and influential in modern science fiction and fantasy literature." His novels include *A Funeral for the Eyes of Fire*; *No Enemy But Time*; *Who Made Stevie Cry?*; *Philip K. Dick Is Dead, Alas*; *Unicorn Mountain*; *Brittle Innings*; and *Joel-Brock the Brave and the Valorous Smalls*. His awards include the Shirley Jackson Award, the Mythopoeic Award, the Nebula Award (twice), the SF Chronicle Award (twice), and the Phoenix Award. He has published over ten short story collections, and his story "Dogs' Lives" was reprinted in *Best American Short Stories*.

Terry Bisson is the author of novels such as *Fire on the Mountain*, *Voyage to the Red Planet*, *The Pickup Artist*, *Planet of Mystery*, and *Any Day Now*. His short fiction has appeared in *Playboy*, *Asimov's*, *Omni*, *Fantasy & Science Fiction*, *Nature*, *Harper's*, and *Tor.com*. One of the premiere writers of short fiction in the field, his stories have won two Nebulas, a Hugo, and two Locus Awards.

John Crowley's novels include *The Deep*, *Beasts*, *Endless Things*, *Engine Summer*, *Little Big*, *Aegypt*, *Four Freedoms*, *The Translator*, *Love and Sleep*, *Daemonomania*, and *Ka: Dar Oakley in the Ruin* *of Ymr*. He has won the Mythopoetic Award (twice), the World Fantasy Award (three times), the *Grand Prix de l'Imaginaire*, and the American Academy Award for Arts and Literature. He is also the recipient of an Ingram Merrill Foundation Grant.

Paul Di Filippo is the author of hundreds of short stories, which have been collected in *The Steampunk Trilogy, Ribofunk, Fractal Paisleys, Lost Pages, Little Doors, Strange Trades, Babylon Sisters*. His novels include *Ciphers, Joe's Liver, Fuzzy Dice, A Mouthful of Tongues*, and *Spondulix*. He has won the British Science Fiction Award and the *Grand Prix de l'Imaginaire*, and has been a finalist for the Hugo, Nebula, BSFA, Philip K. Dick, *Wired Magazine*, and World Fantasy awards.

Andrew Enstice is a scriptwriter, producer, director, and academic who has taught at various universities. He was awarded a scholarship to Emmanuel College, Cambridge, graduating MA, and holds a PhD from Exeter University. His first book, *Landscapes of the Mind* remains the definitive study of Thomas Hardy's literary landscapes in his Wessex books; his play about the nineteenth-century Victorian gold rush premiered in Melbourne. His most recent book is *The Five Star Republic* (co-authored with Janeen Webb, 2021). He is the recipient of numerous awards, including the Bridport Prize for poetry.

William Gibson is an American-Canadian author who has been credited with pioneering the SF subgenre known as cyberpunk. He also coined the term cyberspace in his story "Burning Chrome." His novels include *Neuromancer, Count Zero, Mona Lisa Overdrive, Virtual Light, Idoru, Pattern Recognition, The Peripheral, Agency*, and *The Difference Engine* with Bruce Sterling. His story "Johnny Mnemonic" was made into a film by the same name starring Keanu Reeves and Dolph Lundgren. Gibson is the winner of the *SF Chronicle* Award, the Ditmar Award, the Nebula Award, the Philip K. Dick Award, the Seiun Award, and the Prix Aurora Award (twice). He is also the recipient of the 2019 Grand Master Nebula Award.

Lisa Goldstein's novels include *Ivory Apples; A Mask for the General; Strange Devices of the Sun and Moon; The Dream Years; Dark Cities Underground; Summer King, Winter Fool; Tourists;*

Walking the Labyrinth; and *Weighing Shadows*. Her novel *The Red Magician* won a National Book Award, and her novel *The Uncertain Places* won the Mythopoeic Fantasy Award for Adult Literature. Her short story "Paradise Is a Walled Garden" won the Sidewise Award for Best Short-Form Alternate History.

Richard Harland is an English science fiction and fantasy writer living in New South Wales. He has been an academic, performance artist, and writer. He has written the following critically acclaimed fiction series of novels: *The "Vicar," Eddon & Vail*, *The Heaven and Earth* trilogy, *The Wolf Kingdom*, and *Worldshaker*. He has also written the young adult novels *Walter Wants to Be a Werewolf* and *Sassycat: The Night of the Dead*. His novels, short stories, and children's books have won six Aurealis Awards, including a Golden Aurealis for Best Novel for *The Black Crusade*.

Charlaine Harris is a #1 *New York Times* bestselling author, who has been a published writer for over forty years. Her work has appeared in thirty-odd languages. Her series include the *Aurora Teagarden* mysteries, the *Lily Bard* mysteries, the *Sookie Stackhouse* urban fantasies, the *Midnight, Texas* novels, the *Cemetery Girl* graphic novels (with Christopher Golden), and the *Gunnie Rose* books, set in an alternate history America. The *True Blood* television series, based on the *Sookie Stackhouse* novels, ran for seven seasons. Hallmark adapted her books for *The Aurora Teagarden Mystery Movie Series*, and Universal adapted her *Midnight, Texas* novels for television. Together with Toni L. P. Kelber, she has edited seven themed anthologies.

John Kessel is a multi-award-winning author, playwright, anthologist, and science fiction and fantasy critic. His novels include *Freedom Beach* (with James Patrick Kelly), *Good News From Outer Space*, *Corrupting Dr. Nice*, *The Moon and the Other*, and *Pride and Prometheus*. His plays include *A Clean Escape* and *Faustfeathers*, which won the Paul Green Playwright's Prize. He has won the Nebula Award (twice), the James Tiptree, Jr. Award/ Otherwise Award, the Phoenix Award, and the Shirley Jackson Award. He is the co-creator of the acclaimed Sycamore Hill Writers' Workshop, and co-edited with James Patrick Kelly three collections of science fiction short stories: *Feeling Very Strange: The Slipstream*

Anthology, Rewired: The Post-Cyberpunk Anthology, and *The Secret History of Science Fiction.*

Barry N. Malzberg is a playwright, critic, and a prolific author whose iconic metafictional work has been both wildly praised by critics and attacked by proponents of "hard science fiction." His novel *Beyond Apollo* won the first John W. Campbell Award for Best Science Fiction Novel. He is also the recipient of a Schubert Foundation Playwriting Fellowship and the Cornelia Ward Creative Writing Fellowship. His novels include the *Sigmund Freud* fiction series, *Oracle of the Thousand Hands, Screen, The Falling Astronauts, Overlay, In the Enclosure, Herovit's World, The Men Inside, Guernica Night, Galaxies, Chorale, The Running of Beasts* (with Bill Pronzoni), and *Cross of Fire.* He is also the author of the nonfiction titles *Engines of the Night: Science Fiction in the Eighties, Breakfast in the Ruins: Science Fiction in the Last Millennium,* and *The Bend at the End of the Road.*

Christopher Priest is a British novelist whose books include *the Dream Archipelago* and the *H. G. Wells's War of the Worlds Universe* series, *Indoctrinaire, Inverted World, Fugue for a Darkening Island, Affirmation, The Glamour, The Prestige, The Separation, The Adjacent, An American Story,* and *The Evidence.* A film of his novel *The Prestige* was directed by Christopher Nolan and starred Christian Bale and Hugh Jackman. He has won the British Science Fiction Award (three times), the Ditmar Award (twice), the Kurd Lasswitz Prize, the World Fantasy Award, the *Grand Prix de l'Imaginaire*, the Arthur C. Clarke Award, and the John W. Campbell Memorial Award

Bruce Sterling is one of the founders of the science fiction cyberpunk movement. He edited the influential samizdat-style cyberpunk newsletter *Cheap Truth*, and has become an important futurist and blogger on the web. His nonfiction includes *The Hacker Crackdown: Law and Disorder on the Electronic Frontier, Tomorrow Now: Envisioning the Next Fifty Years,* and *Shaping Things.* His fiction oeuvre includes the *Shaper/Mechanist* series and the novels *Schismatrix, Involution Ocean, Island in the Net, The Difference Engine* (with William Gibson), *Heavy Weather, Holy Fire, Zeitgeist, The Zenith Angle, The Caryatids,* and *Love Is Strange: A Paranormal Romance.* He has won the John Campbell

Memorial Award, the SF Chronicle Award (three times), the Hugo Award (twice), the Locus Award (three times), the Arthur C. Clarke Award, and the Hayakawa Award.

Kim Stanley Robinson is the author of the *Mars* trilogy, the *Orange County* series, and *Science in the Capital* series. His other novels include *Icehenge, The Memory of Whiteness, Antarctica, The Years of Rice and Salt, Galileo's Dream, Aurora, New York 2140, Red Moon*, and *The Ministry for the Future*. Tim Krieder wrote that "Kim Stanley Robinson is generally acknowledged as one of the greatest living science-fiction writers" (*The New Yorker*), and Scott Beauchamp has called Robinson's work "the gold standard of realistic, and highly literary science-fiction writing" (the *Atlantic*). A partial list of his awards would include the World Fantasy Award, the Nebula Award (three times), the John W. Campbell Award, the Hugo Award (twice), the Ignotus Award (twice), the Arthur C. Clarke Award for Imagination in Service to Society, the Robert A. Heinlein Award, the Prix Ozone Award, the Selun Award, and the Locus Award (six times)

Mary Rosenblum passed away on March 11, 2018, when the small craft she was piloting crashed near Battle Ground, Washington. She was a science fiction/fantasy and mystery author. Her novels include *The Drylands, Chimera, The Stone Garden, Water Rights*, and *Horizons*. Under the pseudonym Mary Freeman, she wrote *Devil's Trumpet, Deadly Nightshade, Bleeding Heart*, and *Garden View*. Some of her short fiction can be found in her collection *Synthesis and Other Virtual Realities*. She won the Compton Crook Award, the Asimov's Readers' Poll, and the Sidewise Award for Alternate History. This book is dedicated to her memory.

Pamela Sargent's novels include *Cloned Lives, The Sudden Star, Watchstar, The Golden Space, The Alien Upstairs, Eye of the Comet, Homesmind, Alien Child, The Shore of Women, Venus of Dreams, Venus of Shadows, Child of Venus, Ruler of the Sky*, and *Climb the Wind*. She is the author of the YA *Seed* trilogy (*Earthseed, Farseed*, and *Seed Seeker*). *Earthseed* is currently in development by Paramount Pictures. She is the editor of the *Women of Wonder* anthologies, the first collections of science fiction by women. She has won the Nebula Award and the Locus Award, and was honored with the SFRA Award for Lifetime Contributions to Science Fiction and Fantasy Scholarship (previously the Pilgrim Award) by the Science Fiction Research Association.

Although **Lewis Shiner** has been an important influence on the science fiction genre—he has been called "one of the original cyberpunk authors"—his work is too diverse to fit into any single category. His novels include *Outside the Gates of Eden, Dark Tangos, Black & White, Say Goodbye: the Laurie Moss Story, Glimpses, Slam, Deserted Cities of the Heart*, and *Frontera*. His short fiction can be found in his collections such as *Heroes and Villains, Widows and Orphans: Leftovers by Lewis Shiner, Collected Stories, Love in Vain, The Edges of Things*, and *Nine Hard Questions About the Nature of the Universe*. He is a recipient of the World Fantasy Award.

Mark Shirrefs is an Australian screenwriter who has created, written, story produced, and edited live action and animated television shows such as *The Girl from Tomorrow, Spellbinder, Let the Blood Run Free, Pig's Breakfast, Conspiracy 365, The Adventures of Figaro Pho*, and *Mako Mermaids*. He has taught writing at RMIT University and was a script assessor for the Australian Writers' Guild, Film Victoria, Screen Queensland, and Screen Tasmania. He has won three AWGIE awards for screenwriting; and his credits also include the screenplay for the animated film *The Mysterious Geographic Explorations of Jasper Morello*, which was nominated for an Academy Award. He was the story producer and writer for *The Bureau of Magical Things* television series, which won an ACTAA award in 2018.

Michael Swanwick has received the Hugo, Nebula, Theodore Sturgeon, and World Fantasy Awards for his work. *Stations of the Tide* was honored with the Nebula Award and was also nominated for the Hugo and Arthur C. Clarke Awards. "The Edge of the World," was awarded the Theodore Sturgeon Memorial Award in 1989. It was also nominated for both the Hugo and World Fantasy Awards. "Radio Waves" received the World Fantasy Award in 1996. "The Very Pulse of the Machine" received the Hugo Award in 1999, as did "Scherzo with Tyrannosaur" in 2000. His books include *In the Drift; Vacuum Flowers, Griffin's Egg; Stations of the Tide; The Iron Dragon's Daughter*, which was a *New York Times* Notable Book; and *Jack Faust*. His short fiction has been collected in *Gravity's*

Angels, *A Geography of Unknown Lands*, *Moon Dogs*, *Tales of Old Earth*, and a collection of short-shorts, *Cigar-Box Faust and Other Miniatures*. He lives in Philadelphia with his wife, Marianne Porter, and their son, Sean.

Harry Turtledove is a prolific, multi-award-winning author especially known for his breakthrough counterfactual fiction. His novels include *Guns of the South*, *Thessalonica*, *The Man with the Iron Head*, *Alpha and Omega*, and *Salamis*. His novel series include *Agent of Byzantium*, *Bill Williamson*, *CoDominium Universe*, *Crosstime Traffic*, *Videssos*, *The War That Came Early*, *Darkness*, *Worldwar Universe*, *The Hot War*, and *The Fantastic Civil War*. He has won the Hugo Award, the HOMer Award, the Sidewise Award for Alternate History (three times), the Golden Duck Award, the Prometheus Award, and the Dragon Award.

Howard Waldrop is known primarily for his brilliantly inventive short fiction, which can be found in collections such as *Howard Who?*, *All About Strange Monsters of the Recent Past*, *Night of the Cooters*, *Going Home Again*, *Dream Factories and Radio Pictures*, *Custer's Last Jump and Other Collaborations*, *Heart of Whiteness*, *Horse of a Different Color: Stories*, and *Things Will Never Be the Same: A Howard Waldrop Reader*. His novels include *Them Bones* and *The Texas-Israeli War* (with Jake Saunders). He has won the World Fantasy Award (twice), the Nebula Award, and the Locus Award. His short story "Night of the Cooters" is in production as a short film directed by and starring *Men in Black* actor Vincent D'Onofrio and produced by George R. R. Martin.

Janeen Webb is a multiple-award-winning author, editor, critic, and academic who has written or edited a dozen books and over a hundred essays and short stories. Her most recent novels are *The Gold-Jade Dragon* (2020) and *The Five Star Republic* (co-authored with Andrew Enstice, 2021). She has taught at various universities, is internationally recognized for her critical work in speculative fiction, and has contributed to most of the standard reference texts in the field. She holds a PhD from the University of Newcastle, NSW, and she is a recipient of the World Fantasy Award, the Peter MacNamara SF Achievement Award, the Australian Aurealis Award, and four Ditmar Awards.

George Zebrowski has written or edited over forty books, which include novels, short fiction collections, anthologies, and nonfiction. He has published about a hundred works of short fiction and more than a hundred and forty articles and essays, and has written about science for *Omni Magazine*. His short fiction and essays have appeared in *Analog, Asimov's Science Fiction, Amazing Stories, The Magazine of Fantasy & Science Fiction, Science Fiction Age, Nature*, and the *Bertrand Russell Society News*. His novels include *Macrolife*, which Arthur C. Clarke described as "a worthy successor to Olaf Stapledon's *Star Maker*"; *Stranger Suns*, a *New York Times* Notable Book of the Year; *The Killing Star* (with Charles Pellegrino); *Brute Orbits*; *Cave of Stars*; *Empties*; the *Sunspacers* trilogy; the *Omega Point* trilogy; and *The Star Web*. His awards include the John W. Campbell Memorial Award for Best Science Fiction Novel and the Kevin O'Donnell Jr. Service to SFWA Award.

#

I would like to thank the following people for their help and support:

Veny Armanno, Sophie Beardsworth, John Birmingham, Michael Bishop, Terry Bisson, Paul Brandon, my perspicacious editor Lucy Brown, Sarah Calderwood, Michael Cassutt, John Clute, John Crowley, Rebecca Eskildsen, Paul Di Filippo, Andrew Enstice, William Gibson, Nick Gevers, Stuart Glover, Lisa Goldstein, Martha Grenon, Joe and Gay Haldeman, Richard Harland, Charlaine Harris, Merrilee Heifetz, Gerry Huntman, John Kessel, Barry N. Malzberg, David McDonald, Lee Modesitt, Jr., Steve Paulsen, Gillian Pollock, Christopher Priest, Bruce Sterling, Kim Stanley Robinson, Mary Rosenblum, Nate and Jake Rosenblum, Pamela Sargent, Lewis Shiner, Mark Shirrefs, Stephanie Smith, Jonathan Strahan, Darko Suvin, Michael Swanwick, Dena Bain Taylor, Sudhagaran Thandapani, Angela Tuohy, Harry Turtledove, Janeen Webb, Howard Waldrop, Kim Wilkins (literary and scholarly maven!), Sean Williams, Gary Wolfe, and George Zebrowski.

And I would also like to thank the Graduate School of the University of Queensland for its ongoing support.

INDEX